KYLE MARTIN is contagious! It is clear that in *Reviving the Church*, revival is found more in the reality of an apartment maintenance man than the theology class of the seminary he attended. God's vision and timeless truth meets America. The life change Kyle describes is encouraging, challenging and most of all tangible. The real life stories take a seemingly outdated concept and make it real, relevant, and oh so desirable. God's timeless truth rockets into 21st Century America and we see once again God's abundant life become contagious!

Kenn Kington
Founder of the Ultimate Comedy Theater

This is a different book about revival. It has good research and suggestions but it's personal. Because Kyle shares from his own life, revival becomes attainable rather than just theory.

Roger Cross
President Emeritus, Youth For Christ/USA

REVIVING *the* CHURCH

Keep on pursuing after the Lord!

Hosea 6:1-3

REVIVING *the* CHURCH

everyday theology from a maintenance man's perspective

KYLE LANCE MARTIN

TATE PUBLISHING *& Enterprises*

This title is also available as a Tate Out Loud product. Visit www.tatepublishing.com for more information.

Published by Tate Publishing & Enterprises, LLC
127 E. Trade Center Terrace | Mustang, Oklahoma 73064 USA
1.888.361.9473 | www.tatepublishing.com

Tate Publishing is committed to excellence in the publishing industry. The company reflects the philosophy established by the founders, based on Psalm 68:11,
"The Lord gave the word and great was the company of those who published it."

Cover design by Lynly D. Taylor
Interior design by Kellie Southerland

Published in the United States of America

ISBN: 978-1-60247-856-5
1. Christian Living: Spiritual Growth 2. Spiritual Formation/Prayer
3. Church & Ministry: Church Growth & Church Renewal
4. Evangelism & Outreach
07.12.18

DEDICATION

to laura kim
my wife and best friend for life,
thank you for walking
hand-in-hand with me through the
seasons of our spiritual journey…

ACKNOWLEDGEMENT

"It is good to give thanks to the Lord and sing praises to Your name, O Most High."[1]

When my sister, Janaé, got married, I don't think she could have guessed how much time she and her family would be spending with me during the next ten years. I lived with Janaé and her husband, Garth, during two Texas summers, and Laura and I became weekly visitors when we came to Dallas for seminary. I'm positive that Garth had no idea, after having helped me to clean-up a few college papers, that I would ask him to be my developmental editor for *Reviving the Church.* My close proximity to Garth and Janaé and their little ones, Kade, Lily and Jax, has given them a unique understanding of what I am trying to accomplish. So, when I painted a personal story on paper, Garth was able to interpret what we call "Kyle-isms," and put them into a more reader-friendly structure. Nothing I can say or do will ever show enough gratitude for all that Garth has done during the past year, except to say thanks for your patience, perseverance, and selflessness as you worked on this project. Way to go, G-cat!

With this writing project being a first for me, I would like to express my gratitude to Susan Chaudoir, a former tenant of Swissaire Apartments. With her background and experience in editing, I am ever grateful for her infamous "red pen." She took my maintenance man memoirs and made them easier to read and grammatically correct. Thanks, Susan!

Aside from those directly involved with the editing process, I would like to thank my pastor and friend, Hal Habecker of Dallas Bible Church. Our instant bond as alumni of Taylor University and Dallas Theological Seminary aside, Hal's support and encouragement has always been right on time. Many days when the maintenance work got monotonous, Hal made a perfectly-timed effort to schedule a breakfast or lunch. Whether it was his listening ear or insightful advice, Hal was, and continues to be, very instrumental in my pursuit of revival not only for Dallas Bible Church, but also for the city of Dallas. Can I get an amen?

My brother Shannon doesn't live here in Texas, but the advent of the cell phone has made that fact insignificant. I talked to Shan each and every day during the writing process. I had more writer's block than one single person should ever have but, thanks to big brother, I was able to venture away from the writing mindset and be a part of the Ace Hardware team in Indiana. Shannon and I discussed everything, from his stories of mutually-known customers to the sales for the day. If we weren't talking hardware, we were encouraging one another in this thing we call *life*. Shannon, Have a Nice Day!

My parents, Larry and Gloria, raised me as a Christian and have always been instrumental in my life. From the first time they encouraged me to have a "backyard library" or to participate in the Young Authors' Conference, their love and support has been unconditional. They let me dream. They let me live. They never quenched my heart's desire. Thanks, Dad and Mom!

Finally, I want to acknowledge my wife, Laura, for her faithful role in supporting the path the Lord has placed us on. Whether at 5:03 in the morning, or at midnight, Laura's genuine heart and complete honesty was a never-ending source of encouragement. During our many walks down Swiss Avenue, she was always there to discuss my random thoughts. With "strength and dignity as her clothing,"[2] Laura has been a ongoing blessing to me. I love you, Laura, and I thank you, for everything.

And, of course, I can't forget my little girls—Maya and Nadia. I am so thankful for the both of them, and how they constantly bring a smile to my face. Thanks for being my little buddies!

Of course, there are many others that I want to thank for their prayers and support: Loren and Sue Burket (my praying in-laws), and their dedicated PPN group in Minneapolis. Nikki and the Middlebury Martin kids (supportive sister-in-law and fun loving Regan and Jovi), Sarah and the Johnson family in Colorado (in-laws), the newly-married Burkets in Indianapolis (in-laws), Dr. Walt Baker (faithful mentor and professor at Dallas Theological Seminary), Randy Marshall (teacher and encourager from Dallas Bible Church), Gary and Robin Poplawski (owners of Swissaire Apartments), the neighbors and friends from Swissaire Apartments, the elders and members of Dallas Bible Church, Doug Gibson and the TIME Ministries family, the pastors and congregation of the

Middlebury Church of the Brethren, the crew and campers from Miracle Camp, Dr. Tom Jones (professor at Taylor University), Craig and Megan Barone (friends for life), Mel Domsten (family friend forever), Dave Perkins (buddy from Omaha), FODE House Boys (roommates from college), Troy Tiberi (phone pal from Washington), Sarah Severns (encouraging sister in Christ), Russ and Vanessa Whitfield (adventurous Dallas friends), the workers at Lakewood Ace Hardware (always helping out the maintenance man), Jason Storie and Jared York (former Thursday morning accountability partners from Dallas Bible Church), the Crossroads ABF of Dallas Bible Church, the Prayer Team of Dallas Bible Church (faithful prayer warriors), and Tate Publishing for believing in me enough to make the dream a reality!

TABLE *of* CONTENTS

FOREWORD

Kyle Martin has written a compelling plea urging Christians in America to take God seriously and to open their minds and hearts to the winds of revival that will restore their relationship with Him and renew them in soul. Like John writing to the church in Ephesus, Kyle reminds us that that we have forsaken our "first love" and are in desperate need of revival. He calls on us to "repent and do the things you did at first" (Revelation 3:5b). This counsel comes at a critical time for the church in America.

The personal message of hope and joy developed in this book come from personal experiences with spiritual revival that have been part of Kyle's faithful journey with God. I had the pleasure of teaching a U.S. history survey course in which Kyle was enrolled as a student at Taylor University (Upland). Kyle was particularly interested in our studies of the "Great Awakenings" in American history. His interest was piqued after the Holy Spirit inspired a brief revival among students on the Taylor campus during the spring of 2001. The revival provoked several spirited class discussions during which we revisited the defining characteristics and effects of revival among 18th and 19th century American frontier churches.

The revival that came to campus prior to Easter break in 2001 continues to influence students and faculty who were at its epicenter. Kyle was one of the students through whom God moved in a special way during the revival. His life as a property manager, seminary student, and devoted husband and father testify to the lasting effects of that brief revival on his dreams and deeds. He has a hunger and thirst to know God more deeply and to serve Him more fully. As he writes: "I want to be *Restored.* I want to know and experience the Lord. This is my desire and this desire must become a reality ... everyday."

You can know with certainty that the book you are about to read comes from a genuine disciple of Jesus Christ. It is not a how-to approach to revival. It is not an intellectual study of revival. It is an invitation from a humble servant of God to join him in "a passionate, daily pursuit of the Lord" that will restore and refresh us in mind and soul. As you read, you are invited to discover God anew and to be transformed by taking God seriously each day, acting "upon the direction given to us by the Lord."

As one of Kyle Martin's former professors, I am challenged by his study of revival and his plea for Christians in America to humbly and honestly seek spiritual renewal through a restoration of their faith in God. I am inspired by his call to move beyond revival "as short periods of emotional highs" to experience a deeper relationship with God in which He brings "a natural integration of our beliefs into our daily lives."

I believe that God will use this book to transform your spiritual life if you heed the author's plea: "O Sovereign God, Revive us; restore us; renew us. Turn Your people back to You—so that we may live before You, O God, To know and experience Your presence."

Dr. Thomas Jones
Dean of Arts & Science
Taylor University

the BACKDROP

Dallas, Texas, is not the big city I thought it was when I decided to come here to attend seminary. To clarify, it's one of the bigger cities in the U.S., but it's nowhere near the size of New York, Chicago, Los Angeles or even Washington, D.C. Unlike the skyline of the Big Apple, with its cloud-stabbing skyscrapers stretching on as far as the eye can see, all of the downtown Dallas skyline can be captured in one snap of a photographer's camera.

Dallas, like most metropolitan areas, has its "ghettos" and its run-down neighborhoods. It also has its gated communities that house the area's financial elite. A majority of the economic classes live in very separate areas, on "opposite sides of the tracks" as the saying goes. The area of Dallas that I live in is different. It seems confused. Low-rent apartments and lower-income housing lay a stone's throw away from historical, renovated million-dollar homes. I live and work at an apartment complex off of Swiss Avenue that combines this confusion nicely. The rent is low, with many residents on fixed incomes who have lived there well over twenty years, and the building is historic ... but the complex is far from renovated and can not be confused for the high-priced homes down the street. I am the property manager and maintenance man at this apartment complex and my responsibilities can be quite a challenge. I never really know what kind of repairs or other projects each day will bring. My only sense of normality occurs each morning when I enter my maintenance shop. Here, neatly hung on the back wall, is a message of encouragement to help me keep the attitude of a humble servant. I've deliberately positioned an old flexible desk lamp to illuminate the thick, bold, black letters on a large white canvas. Every morning I enter and read the words of Asaph, "He also chose David His servant and took him from the sheepfolds; from the care of the ewes with suckling lambs He brought him to shepherd Jacob His people, and Israel His inheritance. So he shepherded them according to the integrity of his heart, and guided them with his skillful hands."[4]

Just as King David first served as a shepherd in the fields, I believe the Lord has placed me in this position as preparation. At any time, He will call me from this "pasture of apartments" to serve and guide others with a much broader purpose. With the staff of a shepherd hand, I feel led to encourage a nation-wide time of restoration for the church in America, and believe this is the current path the Lord calls me to follow.

The time is now. It is time for me to sit down in the maintenance shop and articulate what has been placed on my heart and soul. As Habakkuk was instructed to write to the Israelites, I too feel compelled to address the church in America. As I sit in the green plastic chair, I must "write it out in big block letters so that it can be read on the run."[5] The words must be understood. The thoughts must be applicable. The body of Christ in America needs depth, yet they need practicality. Therefore, please hear my cry to the Lord. We can no longer run from what we know to be true. *Let us return to the Lord.* There is no time to spare. Our nation is in a spiritual crisis and we need to be restored. The time is now!

PART I:

REVIVING *the* CHURCH *in* DETAIL

A SERVANT'S REQUEST

a personal plea before the Lord

1. O Lord God, how much longer must You hide Yourself?
As I secretly cry aloud to You in the waking day?

2. O Lord God, how much longer must You wait to reveal Yourself?
As I openly place my thoughts before You in the sleeping night?

3. I ask for restoration, yet quietness continues to surround me.
The world doubts my motives.

4. I wait for a direction, yet nothing is made known.
They question the reality.

5. I pursue a path, yet the light is soft and faint.
And they dispute my reasoning.

6. When will You answer me Lord God?
As Sovereign God, able to examine my innermost being,
You know me better than I know myself;
But when will You answer me Lord God?

7. From the beginning, Your response was already established;
Unfolded with precise sovereignty.

8. Built on commitment and sensitivity,
Your faithfulness was promised to the end.

9. You, O Lord God, instilled in my heart to trust in the past.
Before I sensed Your presence.

10. Convicted my soul to believe in the present
With the faith to live in Your will.

11. And placed in my mind the confidence needed for the future
Knowing You would provide.

12. Deliver me from this dark tunnel of unknown,
And illuminate Your direction for me to serve Your people, O Lord God;

13. According to Your truth,
Lead me to fulfill Your promise,
Yet protect me from the world.

14. Praise be to the Lord God, who will answer my plea for help;

15. I will shout of His goodness and sing of His faithfulness,
For in His sovereignty, He will respond.

16. O Sovereign God,
Revive us; restore us; renew us.

17. Turn Your people back to You—
So we may live before You, O God,
To know and experience Your presence.

18. Day after day, restoration is certain, inevitable and immeasurable.

19. For You, O God, are waiting
To fill the body of Christ with truth and Spirit.

20. As certain as the spring rain,
Pour down upon us, O Lord,
In a season of drought,
We need You.

RESTORATION

My average day on Swiss Avenue might include some light maintenance. I might repair a leaky toilet, grease down the weathered hinges of a tenant's entry door or pick up trash blown from the city streets and scattered along the foundation of our historic red-brick building. Some days, however, require more work. Have I ever told you about apartment #215? A friend and tenant recently moved out of #215, so everything had to be revamped. The apartment needed fresh carpet and new linoleum installed, the walls repainted and the fixtures replaced. Out with the old and in with the new. This is called the "make-ready" process and is simply a part of my job. But, for apartment #215, I knew this would not be enough. No, #215 needed more effort than the same ol' routine. Stains whispered of long-past coffee spills on the cupboards, and the varnish had given in to years of neglect. It was time to restore the worn-down kitchen cabinets. With this project came the guarantee of hard work, lots of sweat, raw knuckles and tons of sawdust. Deep scratch marks traveling in every direction formed a virtual roadmap across the faces of every door and every drawer in apartment #215. I recognized that this was the time for *restoration*.

My life is a lot like apartment #215. After years of neglect and of ignoring the small spills and accidents, it is my job to recognize the need for restoration. But restoration requires the desire to be restored. It must become a priority over other tasks. To restore myself, I must find the desire that often gets lost amidst my human self-centeredness and complacency, scattered and buried in a world of selfishness. It is human nature to address our basic needs first: food, water and shelter. Emotional needs are often second: personal relationships and the giving and receiving of love. Unfortunately, it is our spiritual life that gets put on the backburner. My spiritual life requires Jesus. He is the only one that can fulfill my spiritual needs. He is my desire, yet I often keep Him hidden, buried under many of life's far less important things. *The desire to know and experience the Lord,* it stirs my entire being and this burning desire is only ignited when I turn and look to God.

Moses knew of this desire when he addressed the wandering people of Israel. He said, "If you seek God, your God, you'll be able to find him if you're serious, looking for him with your whole heart and soul."[6] Nothing but the Lord fuels this flame. No matter my human efforts and actions, this desire remains true to itself. Only the Triune God can fulfill this desire. Johann Sebastian Bach, the great music composer, wrote about this kind of desire when he arranged Cantata 147. These lyrics beautifully articulate that the true joy of man's desire is found in Jesus Christ. We are drawn to Him. With Jesus, "the fire of life is impassioned."[7] This desire is deeply embedded through the truth of Jesus Christ and the guidance of the Holy Spirit. And I have to ask myself: "How often do I pursue this desire?" Is this desire a far-distant dream or present actuality? There have been sporadic moments in my life in which I have known and experienced this desire and I recognize that this spiritual inconsistency must come to a halt. I want to be *restored.* I want to know and experience the Lord. This is my desire and this desire must become a reality... everyday.

AWARENESS

As a servant-leader of the Lord, I urge each of you to wholeheartedly reflect on the desire to be *restored.* Do you want to know and experience the Lord in your own life? God is waiting for us to turn from our human ways and return to Him. As He told the Israelites through the prophet Hosea, the Lord will turn from His people until they seek Him. He specifically told the Israelites, "I will go away and return to My place until they acknowledge their guilt and seek My face."[8]

As a lion will return to his lair,[9] God, too, will hide His face from His people, until we confront the guilt and sin surrounding our lives. Hosea pleaded with the Israelites, petitioning his fellow believers, "Let us return to the Lord."[10] God is our one and only God and we must seek Him in earnest. Let our souls thirst for Him. Let our flesh yearn for Him.[11] *Let us return to the Lord.*

Please take this matter personally. Please take this plea seriously. We can no longer afford to ignore God and continue with the actions displayed by the body of Christ. During the past century, the church in America has slowly lost the desire to know Christ and experience Him in truth and spirit. Unfortunately, it's overwhelmingly as obvious as the stains and scratched cabinets of apartment #215. When a conflict or disagreement arises in a church, the easiest solution is to attend another church. Maybe try another denomination: Baptist, Methodist, perhaps Catholic, Pentecostal, Brethren, or Bible. The movement from one church to another based on petty things create a confused and ugly map, much like the kitchen cabinet drawer-faces in #215 ... a busy map of scratches leading nowhere.

> We see the same in Christian marriages. When the going gets tough, why not divorce? According to the Barna Group, "Among married born again Christians, 35% have experienced a divorce. That figure is identical to the outcome among married adults who are not born again: 35%."[12] *What about the affirmation of homosexuality in the church?* The Barna Group reported, 34% [of born-again believers] said homosexual relations should be considered legal.[13] *What about abortion?* Since the Supreme Court's ruling in *Roe vs. Wade* on January 22, 1973, an estimated 46 million babies were killed through the process of abortion. Statistically, one baby is aborted every 24 seconds.[14] W*hat about the problems of poverty and AIDS*? Can we honestly say we have helped the poor, like Lazarus,[15] or assisted the ten lepers[16] of the 21st Century? Over 1 billion people (one-sixth of the world's population) live in extreme poverty (defined as living on less than $1 a day).[17] There are 38 million people currently infected and living with AIDS. Are we doing anything to help those affected by this epidemic?[18]

As I tend to the daily maintenance calls around these old apartments, I often smile when I catch a glimpse of a steeple that adorns the roof of this old building. We actually have several white steeples on the roof and they often stir feelings that I serve as a "pastor" to the people who live here. Aside from staining cabinets and painting the apartments, my job is to serve and meet the personal needs of the tenants. This wasn't part of the job description when I was hired but, please, tell me of an actual job description that encompasses everything that the job entails. There isn't one. *Reality requires our lives to be flexible.* I realize the importance of this, which is why I make myself available to those in need. Even in this apartment complex, where the majority of individuals are believers, the needs and issues are endless. Sometimes too many for me to personally handle, but the Lord has called me to help bring restoration to *these* people—His people—who live on Swiss Avenue in Dallas, Texas.

One tenant in particular comes to mind. As a recent graduate of the nearby seminary, this man named Joe had, at one time, a desire to serve the Lord. It was unclear how he might serve, but Joe knew the Lord wanted him in the ministry. Over a two-month period, my wife and I observed some unusual behavior by this man. He would exit through the front of our complex and walk to the street where he would lean into the passenger-side window of a rough-looking car with black-tinted windows. He didn't seem to approach as a friend and only talked briefly with the vehicle's two occupants before returning quickly to his apartment. Something was not right. Whenever I approached him he was distant and disinterested.

We were concerned for Joe. As apartment managers, we had an obligation to pursue this issue if other tenants' safety was at risk. Moreover, as fellow believers, we cared for his walk with the Lord. So we began to pray about the issue and it didn't take long for the Lord to answer. One Sunday night, we got a call from the entry phone box that is mounted on the front stoop of our apartments. It was Joe and he didn't have his keys to his apartment. After a long discussion, he explained that he was thrown in jail and his car had been impounded. He was charged with a felony for possession of cocaine and a misdemeanor for possession of a crack pipe. Not your seminary graduate's typical excuse for losing their keys. Joe was an addict.

Over time, I prayed about restoration within Joe's life. Yet, he wasn't ready. He wasn't willing. His drug use continued. He lost his job. He refused to go to rehabilitation. He knew what he was doing but didn't see the consequences. He was running from the Lord and had no desire to turn to Him. It was getting worse. Eventually, I told him that if he didn't go to rehab and get help, I would evict him based on the illegal activities taking place in his apartment.

Finally, fear kicked in for Joe ... temporarily. Joe agreed to go to rehab. Before he left, he came into the office, and we prayed and discussed a passage from one of the minor prophets of the Old Testament. In the book of Hosea, the people of Israel had turned their back on God, but the prophet Hosea exclaimed that restoration could—and would—occur for each of them, *if* they were willing to return to the Lord. The prophet pleaded:

> Come let us return to the Lord. For He has torn us, but He will heal us; He has wounded us, but He will bandage us. He will revive us after two days; He will raise us up on the third day, that we may live before Him. So let us know, let us press on to know the Lord. His going forth is as certain

> as the dawn; and He will come to us like the rain,
> like the spring rain watering the earth.[19]

Joe acknowledged the truth about this Scripture and how it applied to his life. He knew he needed to turn to the Lord. So he folded the paper I had printed the verse on, placed it in his back pocket, and headed off to the rehab center ... or so he said. Two days went by and neither I nor the rehab center heard from Joe. We were concerned. He didn't have a cell phone and we had no way of communicating with him. So we engaged in intercessory prayer on Joe's behalf. Soon enough, the Lord answered again.

One afternoon, Joe showed up at our apartments. I was working on some vertical blinds in a tenant's kitchen when he passed me. Oops! He didn't know I was there. Quickly, I dropped everything and stopped him. This twenty-minute, one-way conversation was what I would classify as "tough love." Either he went to get help, for a minimum of thirty days, starting that night, or he would be evicted within seventy-two hours. Even though Joe was a believer, I couldn't stand for this. He needed to be free from his addiction. He needed to be restored in his relationship with the Lord. But the problem, which he admitted to, was that he hadn't hit rock bottom yet. He had gone through thousands of dollars for drugs, been thrown in jail, lost his job, and yet he still wasn't at his wit's end. The desire for restoration had to come from within, and at that moment in his life, it wasn't there.

IMPLEMENTATION

Believers in America must recognize that, like the Israelites of Hosea's era, we have placed ourselves on a path to self-destruction. This recognition brings awareness. And this awareness is the kindling used to ignite the fire of restoration. A passionate, daily pursuit of the Lord fans the flames which rapidly spread genuine restoration.

The prophet Hosea agreed, "So let us know, let us press on to know the Lord."[20] He called the nation of Israel to chase after God with a new devotion.[21] In America, we must do the same. As the body of Christ, we must pursue, renew, and refresh our allegiance with the Lord.[22] With all of our heart, all of our soul, all of our mind and all of our strength, a restoration from the Lord *is* possible.

But let's be real. If we took a survey, could we honestly say that we are *actively* pursuing the Lord in truth and spirit, or are we standing still, stuck in the stagnant ways of church routine? The apostle Paul encouraged us to choose the devoted Christian lifestyle when he wrote, "Therefore I, the prisoner of the Lord, implore you to walk in a manner worthy of the calling with which you have been called, with all humility and gentleness, with patience, showing tolerance for one another in love, being diligent to preserve the unity of the Spirit in the bond of peace."[23] It is up to each of us to "walk" in such a manner.

How do we learn this walk? First, we need to reestablish ourselves in the Word of God. Unfortunately, we have a tendency to quietly ignore the truth. This is especially true when we are placed in busy and fast-paced environment and we simply don't make the time to read the Bible. But to deny the Word of God from speaking into our lives is unacceptable. We must use Scripture as the measuring stick for our everyday life. George Barna wrote, "Exposure to the Bible clearly affects a person's views on these matters. It seems that if... Christians have any chance of restoring a more traditional moral perspective to America, it is most likely to be accomplished by encouraging people to base their moral choices on the basis of God's Word rather than on the basis of cultural leanings or political arguments."[24] So, as American believers, when we stray from the truth or unknowingly act contrary to Scripture, what should we do? Allow me to state the obvious—*we must get back into the Word of God in order for our lives to be measured by the absolute standard.* This is what I did in regards to the issue of salvation. *(Please refer to Appendix I for an example of how I personally used the Bible to be better equipped.)*

Aside from our own personal studies, we must hold one another accountable, encouraging each other to engage in the Word of God. We must do this because there is "an essential link between knowing God's Word and applying it to one's daily life."[25] Respected author and theologian H. Wayne House wrote, "Right doctrine should produce right practice."[26] The apostle Paul confirmed this purpose of Scripture to his friend and fellow believer Timothy, "All Scripture is inspired by God and profitable for teaching, for reproof, for correction, for training in righteousness; so that the man of God may be adequate, equipped for every good work."[27]

Not only is our obedience to absolute truth on the decline, but the body of Christ in America is also noticeably less reliant on the Holy Spirit's guidance. As an example, think about your own walk with the Lord. Close your eyes and answer these questions honestly: How often do you obey the powerful whispers of the Holy Spirit? Do you realize that the truth of the gospel came not only through the Word, but also by the means of the Holy Spirit?[28] When we first came to faith in Jesus, we chose to listen to and obey the "full conviction"[29] of the Holy Spirit. It is now time for the body of Christ in America to listen again to the Spirit. Jesus emphasized the importance of the Holy Spirit when He said, "But the Helper, the Holy Spirit, whom the Father will send in My name, He will teach you all things, and bring to your remembrance all that I said to you."[30] On a daily basis, the Spirit is present to provide spiritual insight for our lives.[31] The Spirit allows us to passionately tap into a personal relationship with the Lord, and the result of living a Spirit-filled life is a plethora of fruit for all to see.[32]

Let's go back to Joe the addict. He continued to turn his back on the Lord for weeks. Then, one day, whether it was because of reminders from the Word of God, the powerful presence of the Holy Spirit, relentless prayer, the persistence of my wife and I, the love of another caring individual or the threat of going to jail, Joe finally decided to look for help. And, he did it himself. It had to come from his inner desire and will to change. Joe was determined to implement the process of restoration for his own life. He wanted to change. He wanted to get help. He acknowledged that the sin of cocaine use had complete control over his life, and he needed help from God and others.

So, over the course of three months, Joe pressed on. He poured himself into the rehabilitation center. He wanted to experience the recovery process to its fullest. He took it seriously. He had no job during this time. He forked out thousands of dollars for the finest treatment. He began to pray again. He began to read Scripture again. He began to worship the Lord in "truth and spirit."[33] He knew he needed to do what it would take to get better.

Amazingly, Joe soon became a recognized and respected leader within the community of addicts. Even to the extent that he was appointed "mayor" over the other individuals. Within the rehab center, Joe was overcoming his addiction. He was becoming restored in the Lord.

IMPACT

Let's embrace it! The body of Christ in America can *experience* restoration. It starts with awareness of our spiritual mindset. When we turn this awareness into everyday action, our lives will be transformed by God. Like the prophet Hosea wrote, "As certain as the dawn; and He will come to us like the rain, like the spring rain watering the earth."[34] God is waiting for us to call upon Him. He is prepared to pour out His blessings upon His people, a sign of the Lord's favor in our lives. Moses spoke to this:

> But the land into which you are about to cross to possess it, a land of hills and valleys, drinks water from the rain of heaven, a land for which the Lord your God cares; the eyes of the Lord your God are always on it, from the beginning even to the end of the year. It shall come about, If you listen obediently to my commandments which I am commanding you today, to love the Lord your God and to serve Him with all your heart and all your soul, that He will give the rain for your land in its season, the early and late rain, that you may gather in your grain and your new wine and your oil. He will give grass in your fields for your cattle, and you will eat and be satisfied.[35]

When the Lord serves as our source of restoration, according to His will and timing, we possess a blessed assurance that He will work in our lives. And when others witness God provide our every need, our lives influence and impact everyone around us. Take, for example, Moses' relationship with God. Exodus 34:34–35 said, "But whenever Moses went in before the Lord to speak with Him, he would take off the veil until he came out; and whenever he came out and spoke to the sons of Israel what he had been commanded, the sons of Israel would see the face of Moses, that the skin of Moses' face shone."[36] Others will notice God's influence in our lives. Moses knew this. We, too, must understand that God's reflection in us *will* encourage others to know and experience the warmth of the Lord's blessings.

During our interaction with Joe the addict, Laura and I prayed that he would see the reflection of Christ in our lives. During Joe's time in the rehabilitation center, we attempted to visit him on a weekly basis. We would engage him in conversation about current events, his progress in rehabilitation, and sometimes just mingled with others while sharing a meal and our random thoughts. Laura and I knew that we must be there to encourage him in this process. He needed support. Who doesn't? His progress had been very good. In fact, Joe had been moved up to a level three in his rehab program. What does a level three mean? It means the addictive nature of cocaine was slowly being overcome. Progress was being made. Amen! Joe attended meetings and counseling and talked with others who struggled with the same addictions. Restoration confronts the past in order to make progress in the present and into the future. Joe's restoration was evident. He had renewed his identity in Jesus Christ. Not only had he turned to the Lord for help through prayer and Bible reading, but Joe had taken on a "silent" leadership role within the rehabilitation center. He was impacting lives through his own restoration process. Joe has a long journey ahead of him but, thankfully, it is a journey Joe knows he cannot successfully accomplish without the Lord at his side.

Let's face it; the process of overcoming our sins and struggles in life is difficult. It might not be as difficult as Joe's, but the concept is the same. We are constantly pushing off and delaying the inevitable. But the Lord will be with us in the process of confession and letting go of our past. We must go after the Lord in a new and refreshing manner.

We must stop kidding ourselves that we don't need to be restored. The body of Christ in America must come to terms with our current spiritual health. Must we wait until we hit rock bottom? For who knows what that would actually entail. But one thing is for sure, once we press on to know Him more intimately, His presence will flood into our lives. Our attitudes and actions will reflect our obedience to the working of the Holy Spirit. And, more importantly, because of our own pursuit of restoration, we will encourage others to do the same. The Spirit will fan the flame of restoration within this country.

Disclaimer: Restoration is a never ending process! It doesn't stop once we are in the free-and-clear for a couple of weeks. Our love for God mustn't stop after a one-week emotional high. Restoration must continue throughout our lives … each and every day.

> Restoration distinguishes itself through the process of *humility*. It never stops.
> Restoration reveals itself through the disciplines of *prayer and fasting*. They mustn't stop.
> Restoration discloses itself through the pursuit of *holiness*. It won't stop.
> Restoration announces itself through the *Divine response*. God won't stop.

You see, my friend Joe—he has fallen back into his old lifestyle of drug use. He has turned his back on what he first fell in love with—Jesus. The cocaine has him high once again. He is Joe the addict. The personal restoration process has been locked in the trunk and it will probably remain there until Joe realizes that he must flee the temptations of this world, and more specifically, this neighborhood. Joe's lifestyle of addiction is the direct result of his reliance on his own limited powers and not the powers of the Sovereign Lord. The destination for Joe the addict is one of tragedy. Homelessness, prison, death ... none of the places Joe daydreamed about as a young child. The same goes for the body of Christ in America. We must hold strong, and rely on the Lord for the process of restoration. We need the Lord Almighty to reveal Himself in our lives at all times. Otherwise, the church in America is headed for dire straits.

A SERVANT'S REQUEST

Concentration of humility

21. O Lord God,
Strip our humanity; cleanse our sinfulness.

22. Make it known to us Lord,
When clothed in humility,
The throne of restoration awaits;

23. Where attitudes and actions are emptied,
Reflections of the Bond-Servant are evident,
And selfless-obedience is emulated.

24. Praise the name of God!
Let every voice gather together in unity,
And exalt praise to the One whose name is above all else.

25. For You are worthy of adoration and praise,
From every tribe, tongue, people, and nation.
Praise the name of God!

HUMILITY
In Pursuit of Concentration

Restoration of the kitchen cabinets in apartment #215 was an inexpensive process, but it was labor intensive. Taking off the cabinet doors and hardware begins the beautification procedure. With a palm sander and numerous squares of 60-grit sandpaper, the scratches, stains, and the varnish slowly fade. The old, scarred finish did not disappear immediately, but when the sander came to a stop and the dust settled, all you could see was the beautiful, natural grain of the bare wood. It's a beautiful thing (at least for a carpenter or a maintenance man like me). There is a process to get to this point. Rough sand paper removed all of the old stain. Fine, 220-grit sandpaper removed any marks hiding within the grain. Super fine-grade steel wool pads, gave the "final finish." In the end, the old, battered, scratched, stained and scarred cabinets were wiped "clean."

We must be willing to confront our shortcomings, as they relate to truth and Spirit, in order to see the beauty within the body of Christ. Let us admit as believers in America that we have strayed from the Lord. Restoration begins when we recognize we have turned away from the Lord. God will tune out our requests if we don't recognize we need to change. The psalmist wrote, "If I regard wickedness in my heart, the Lord will not hear."[37] Unfortunately, we learn to rely on our own strengths and abilities. Human self-reliance cannot be an option if we desire to experience restoration. As believers, we need to need Him. But this process of restoration does not come naturally to anyone. As the body of Christ in America, we look for restoration through busyness rather than the original divine source. We figure that if we keep busy "with church" then we must be right with the Lord. It is an unspoken expectation for each and every American to remain active. Within the walls of the churches, Bible studies and prayer times are continued. Potluck dinners are regularly served and songs go on singing. And for this faithfulness we should rejoice? The problem is that we end up substituting these "activities" for a personal relationship with Jesus Christ, using the influences of neither in our daily lives. We sweep issues under the rug. Life is easier when we rely on the comfort of our current lifestyles. Society has trained us to portray our lives as a perfectly-framed picture. Why should we stir the waters when things are floating smoothly? But I ask each of you, is this approached lifestyle typical of first-century believers? Based on the foundation laid by the apostles, the answer is no. Our faithful relationship with the true Messiah is intended to be a personal one. He is waiting for us to draw near to Him, but we have to recognize our own need for restoration. The prophet Jeremiah wrote in his time of sorrow, "Restore us to You, O Lord, that we may be restored; renew our days as of old."[38] In the book *Revivals of Religion*, Charles Finney wrote, "If we need to be revived, it is our duty to be revived. If it is our duty, it is possible."[39] Can you imagine life if we approached all things with this attitude as if we were constantly refreshed by being in the presence of the Lord?

We need to take ownership. We need to live each day with a new and fresh perspective for God. The psalmist referred to this Godly desire when he wrote, "As the deer pants for the water brooks, so my soul pants for You, O God. My soul thirsts for God, for the living God."[40] Imagine what the body of Christ in America would look like if we had this kind of passion for the Lord. Imagine how different and distinct we would be from the world if we actually lived it out. We are a group of individuals chosen to be set apart. The apostle Peter wrote, "But you are the ones chosen by God, chosen for the high calling of priestly work, chosen to be a holy people, God's instruments to do his work and speak out for him, to tell others of the night-and-day difference he made for you—from nothing to something, from rejected to accepted."[41] We are to live with the same faith in Jesus Christ, regardless of our denomination. We are to live with the same hope, regardless of our background. And with this faith and hope, we as the body of Christ are to live as people of love; despite our financial status.

> The body of Christ in America needs to be restored.
> Let us return to the faith we have in God.
> Let us awaken to the hope we have in Jesus Christ.
> Let us fall in love with God and emulate this love for others.
> By the power of the Holy Spirit, let us return to the Lord.

By no means do I think that every believer has fallen to the wayside and forgotten Jesus Christ. There are thousands upon thousands who love the Lord and live out their relationship with Him. The prophet Elijah felt all alone when he faced Baal and the false prophets, yet God confirmed to Elijah that 7,000 people in Israel did not bow to worship the false god.[42] There were others who believed just as Elijah. And for this reason—the desire to see a *unified* faith—I write this book of encouragement. There are people throughout the United States waiting to know these words and experience Him on a more personal level. They simply need a little encouragement. Where faith has been lost, hope misplaced, and love found in all the wrong places, we need to desire to know and experience God more. To come before the Lord in humility brings *restoration* to our lives.

UNDERSTANDING

Restoration can be a demanding process, but all the more rewarding as it takes place. However, nothing will occur unless we are willing to approach God in recognition of the sin in our lives. Bono, a popular Irish preacher cloaked in rock star's clothes, referred to restoration when he wrote:

> I'm not broke but you can see the cracks
> You can make me perfect again
> All because of you
> All because of you
> All because of you
> I am . . . I am
> I'm alive
> I'm being born
> I just arrived, I'm at the door
> Of the place I started out from
> And I want back inside.[43]

As the church in America, we need to humble ourselves and come before the Almighty God. It is time. It is time to recognize that God is ready and willing to rid us of our sinful lifestyles. The prophet Isaiah wrote, "A Message from the high and towering God, who lives in Eternity, whose name is Holy: 'I live in the high and holy places, but also with the low-spirited, the spirit-crushed, and what I do is put new spirit in them, get them up and on their feet again.'"[44]

In this humbling process of restoration, our sins will be exposed like the grain of a freshly sanded wood. When we spend time coming before the Lord, the past will be brought to present. Our sins will be placed on the table. The heartaches will be announced. We must sand ourselves down and strip ourselves of the years of sin and neglect. The first step of the restoration process begins with *humble confession.*

How can we as individuals expect to "maintain the same love, united in spirit, and intent on one purpose"[45] if we hold onto our sins? We cannot. Restoration will always remain distant if we are consumed with ourselves. According to the apostle Paul, when selfishness and conceitedness is present, *we* become the focus and the focus should be on our relationship with Christ. "With humility in mind,"[46] each of us can perform an honest evaluation of our own sinful nature.[47]

King David, upon committing adultery, evaluated his sinful state, and confessed to the Lord that he needed to be cleansed. He realized the evil he had done before the Lord, and pleaded to the Lord:

> Create in me a clean heart, O God, and renew a steadfast spirit within me. Do not cast me away from Your presence and do not take Your Holy Spirit from me. Restore to me the joy of Your

> salvation and sustain me with a willing spirit. Then I will teach transgressors Your ways, and sinners will be converted to you.[48]

Through humble confession, King David had a new sense of appreciation and value for others. The apostle Paul encouraged the people of Israel to do the same as David, and pursue this "self-examination process;"[49] so that they, too, would "be devoted to one another in brotherly love; give preference to one another in honor."[50] Paul further wrote to the church at Philippi, "Regard one another as more important than yourselves; do not merely look out for your own personal interests, but also for the interest of others."[51] When we discard sin in our lives, humility is revealed by our love for the Lord and focus on others. Both are essential to living a sanctified lifestyle.

One day, as I entered the doors of the local Ace Hardware, all I could think about was my personal checklist. I had a written list that included items I needed for the apartment complex, but I also had a mental list that included "items" I needed to get done in life. I had too much going on in my head. How was I going to get it all done? I was feeling stressed. I was overwhelmed. My cell phone was constantly ringing, even as I walked down the electrical aisle. The car was making strange noises again. How long would we live in our two-bedroom apartment? I just wanted to crumple up the list and stop thinking about my personal situation.

Then it hit me. My self-centeredness hit me right in the face. At that moment, I realized I had become inward-focused, and not outward-focused. So, as I approached the counter, all of the apartment-preparation, the seminar-teachings, everything went out the window. My worries, my frets and my thoughts were set aside. I asked God to forgive me. Then I looked up, dropped the electrical outlets on the counter, and began to talk to the grandmother/granddaughter team that worked the cash registers. I sincerely wanted to know how they were both doing. It turns out, the granddaughter just got married over the weekend. Just by finding that out, I was convicted. I was convicted because, if I had not stopped thinking about myself, I would never have known about the life-changing event of the Ace Hardware clerk.

It seems small, yet with just such a personal assessment, the process of the glorification of Jesus Christ can begin.[52] No longer will our selfish ways be the priority; instead, by confessing our shortcomings, Christ will be exalted.

EXEMPLIFY

Through the death, burial, and resurrection of Jesus Christ, our sins are wiped clean. When we understand the absolute need for confession, we begin to exemplify the Lord with a new way of living. In a sermon preached during a revival in Los Angeles, Billy Graham referred to this kind of repentance when he said, "Repentance is confession of sin, repentance is sorrow for sin, and repentance is renouncing sin. Many people believe God's Word and accept Christ's sacrifice, but they have never been truly repentant! If they were, their lives would show it."[53] True confession will reflect the humility of His Son Jesus Christ and lead to a life that brings glory to God who created us.

This humility, specifically mentioned in the apostle Paul's writings to the Philippians, occurs in our lives when we have the attitude of Christ. When the renewing of our minds takes place, that we might be like-minded with Jesus, we are able to spur on a renewal within the whole body of Christ. Paul encouraged the church at Ephesus to have this mindset, when he reminded them what they already knew to be true,

> You learned Christ! My assumption is that you have paid careful attention to him, been well instructed in the truth precisely as we have it in Jesus. Since, then we do not have the excuse of ignorance, everything—and I do mean everything—connected with that old way of life has to go. It's rotten through and through. Get rid of it! And then take on an entirely new way of life—a God-fashioned life, a life renewed from the inside and working itself into your conduct as God accurately reproduces his character in you.[54]

Likewise, we must focus on renewing our minds. Paul wrote, "Therefore I urge you, brethren, by the mercies of God, to present your bodies a living and holy sacrifice, acceptable to God, which is your spiritual service of worship. And do not be conformed to this world, but be transformed by the renewing of your mind, so that you may prove what the will of God is, that which is good and acceptable and perfect."[55] When we do, our actions will reflect our attitudes. When we lie, our attitude misrepresents truth. When we steal, our attitude avoids labor. When we curse, our attitude eludes edification. When we grieve the Spirit, our attitude ignores Divine guidance. When we are unforgiving, our attitude disregards kindness. Attitudes carry out our actions, and reflect our level of humility. The bottom line is, how we view ourselves is how we carry ourselves in front of others.

Jesus Christ "existed in the form of God, (He) did not regard equality with God a thing to be grasped."[56] *(paren-*

theses refer to author input) Even though Christ was the very essence of God Himself, He humbled himself through the incarnation and "embraced perfect humanity.[57]" In other words, Jesus Christ, who was fully God and fully man, set all authority and power aside in order to bring salvation to mankind. Even though it meant that He would be ridiculed, mocked, and scorned. Christ was willing to humble Himself before all mankind. Robert Lightner best described this attitude of humility when he wrote, "Christ did not hesitate to set aside His self-willed use of deity when He became a man. As God He had all the rights of deity, and yet during His incarnate state He surrendered His right to manifest Himself visibly as the God of all splendor and glory."[58] Humility exemplified the life of Christ for He came to serve, not to be served.[59]

Paul confirmed this servant-leadership approach of Christ when he wrote, "But emptied Himself, taking the form of a bond-servant being made in the likeness of men."[60] Christ did not spend His short time on Earth trying to implement His authority as King; on the contrary, He came to establish His earthly role as a servant. Instead of pursuing power and prestige, we are called to a life of service. I am fully aware that this concept is much easier to write about than it is to follow.

With seminary graduation behind me, I feel as if people are waiting—waiting for me to "do something" with my life. It's time for me to move on and get a "real job." I know maintenance work is not glamorous. It doesn't bring in the big bucks. It doesn't exactly convey something that others can get excited about. Most think a Masters degree in Biblical Studies would lead to a job as a pastor, a teacher, or a missionary. To me, however, my seminary degree allows me to impact those around me and integrate the Scriptures into everyday encounters. Not long ago, as

I was changing a light bulb outside apartment #106, I received a phone call. When asked if I was busy, I replied that I was changing a light bulb.

The response from the caller was quick and sarcastic, "Is that why you went to seminary, to change a light bulb?" I don't remember how I replied, but I do remember thinking, "The Lord has provided for all of my family's needs, and then some. I am fully confident that the Lord has me right where He wants me. It doesn't matter what I am doing, as long as I am doing it for the Lord and not myself. I have willingly chosen to give my life for the sake of Jesus Christ."

I know that viewing my post-seminary lifestyle from other's perspectives makes it hard to understand, but I truly believe that the Lord wants me to invest into the community at Swissaire Apartments and that of the surrounding neighborhood. I am simply trying to light up the place with the love of Christ. One morning, while looking out the window, Laura and I saw a homeless man sitting in a lawn chair across the street. Next to him was an empty lawn chair. Seeing a homeless person across from our apartment complex is not abnormal, but seeing two lawn chairs in a parking lot sure was! My wife, knowing me all too well, encouraged me to go out and talk with the man. We both thought he could use some company. So I ventured out to the streets to try and brighten up his day.

As I approached him and all his belongings packed into a single clear briefcase, I realized I knew this homeless man. His name was Tucker. He has been around the area before. Seeing me coming towards him, Tucker offered me the empty lawn chair next to him. I accepted, but before I could sit down, he placed a piece of cardboard on the seat. He didn't want my clothes to get dirty. Even though I was in work clothes and a hat-labeled "maintenance man" (yeah, it literally says *Maintenance Man*), Tucker was thoughtful and concerned.

We got to talking about how long he has been on the streets, and what he does during the day. It wasn't a deep or personal conversation, but I could tell he enjoyed this time of fellowship. People slowly walked by and even tenants of Swissaire gave the two of us some double-takes. Two guys sitting on lawn chairs in a parking lot talking. One looked homeless (he actually was) and one looked like a maintenance man who had just finished replacing a bathroom sink faucet (I actually did).

By my taking the time to come out, I could tell I was making a difference in his life at that moment. It didn't take much. I sat down in the chair, and talked to Tucker. I showed to him that I was interested in *his* life, regardless of how others looked at me. Rough, ragged, torn. It didn't matter to me.

The conversation came to an abrupt halt when a fire engine with lights flashing and sirens screaming stopped in front of our apartments. My managerial instincts kicked in, I said my goodbyes to Tucker, shook his hand, and I went running over to the fire truck. Two firemen headed to the front door. As they turned my way I asked if there was anything I could do to help them. Before they answered, they looked me up and down. Then looked over at Tucker sitting in his lawn chair, and noticing the empty lawn chair I just left. Looking back at me, one fireman asked, "I'm sorry, but can I help you?" I guess they associated me with Tucker and wanted nothing to do with me so I told them I was the manager of the complex and they chuckled. Again, I affirmed that I was the manager here, and would be happy to help them. In order to convince them, I used my front door security code to let them in the complex. Thankfully, there was no fire. In an indirect manner, as they performed a routine inspection, the firemen apologized for the confusion. They were obviously perplexed about me sitting in a parking lot with Tucker the homeless man, yet when we relinquish self-interests, we truly exalt the name of Christ.

SACRIFICE

Whatever it takes, I have decided to give my life for the sake of Jesus Christ. If my job means that I'm a maintenance man, so I can minister to individuals like Tucker, then so be it. It's not a "dream" job, but then again, once we commit to Christ, our lives become His. Regardless of the job titles and scenarios, we are to make ourselves available to love God and love others at all costs, or as Moses wrote, "You shall love the Lord your God with all your heart and with all your soul and with all your might."[61] Nothing is to hold us back. The apostle Paul described Christ's ultimate humility in Philippians 2:8: "Being found in appearance as a man, He humbled Himself by becoming obedient to the point of death, even death on a cross." Christ didn't set personal boundaries for serving others. He didn't have limitations. He accepted His role and willingly obeyed His role from God the Father. He was to die on the cross, be buried, and rise again on the third day so that all of mankind would have the opportunity to be saved and be granted eternal life.

Humility is essential to personal life-transformation and a tough lesson to learn and apply to our own lives. Too many times we come up with excuses. We must overcome waiting for perfect situations in order to glorify God. Right now, we can each make a difference in the body of Christ in America through our obedience to Christ. It might not be in the drastic manner of actually giving up our physical life (as some Christians in other countries), but it might mean giving up comfortable and secure lifestyles. But a little discomfort can make a big difference not only in our lives, but others' lives as well.

One evening around 10:30 p.m., I was walking to the maintenance shop when a tenant called out my name. The tenant had spotted a snake in front of apartment #122's door. My heart sank. Let me explain one thing right away—I, like Indiana Jones, absolutely despise snakes. I'm not too hip on rats, rodents, possums, or any other creepy critter either. So, taking a deep breath, I walked over to the apartment and saw the 2-foot snake curled in a ball. Acting like it was no big deal in front of the tenant, I said I would be right back. I immediately went to my apartment and asked my wife Laura what to do. How do you kill a snake? Thankfully, our good friend Vanessa (whose family was from Argentina) was there. She simply stated that back in her family's country they would take a shovel and beat it to death.

Well, that didn't sound too inviting, but what were my options? I had to kill the snake. Nobody else was jumping up and down to help. Therefore, as the manager, I needed to remain faithful to my responsibilities of keeping the community safe. So I went back to the shop, grabbed the shovel, and walked with confidence. That was, until I was reminded what the snake looked like. With its mouth open, fangs shining in the 60-watt light, and neck perched, nervousness kicked in. That was, until a Bible verse came to mind. Psalm 91:11–13 quietly reassured me:

> For He will give His angels charge concerning you, To guard you in all your ways. They will bear you up in their hands, That you do not strike your foot against a stone. You will tread

upon the lion and cobra, The young lion and
the serpent you will trample down.

Okay, so the snake wasn't a large cobra, but the same concept applies to garter snakes. I was confident I could trample down the serpent. After five drastic shovel chops to the snake, the serpent finally fell limp. The chore wasn't easy. I didn't want to do it, but because of obligation and responsibility, I took on the task. The Lord became my strength when I was weak (specifically in the knees). To me, it was a small form of sacrifice, that doesn't compare, in the least, to persecution, yet with obedience to the task at hand, I gave it my all.

Christ wants our complete and undivided attention. The apostle Paul confirmed this approach to his own life, when he wrote to the Galatians, "I have been crucified with Christ; and it is no longer I who live, but Christ lives in me; and the life which I live in the flesh I live by faith in the Son of God, who loved me and gave Himself up for me."[62]

Thankfully, there is a reason for this humbled form of servant-hood. God will be glorified. The focus will be on Him, and not us. This is a very significant reason and we must praise the Lord for this. Paul agreed when he wrote, "For this reason also, God highly exalted Him, and bestowed on Him the name which is above every name, so that at the name of Jesus every knee will bow, of those who are in heaven and on earth, and that every tongue will confess that Jesus Christ is Lord, to the glory of God the Father."[63]

A SERVANT'S REQUEST

Focus on prayer and fasting

26. O Lord God,
Rend our hearts.
With compassion and lovingkindness,

27. Declare to us Lord,
A blessing is sure to come,
Through fasting, weeping, and mourning.
28. May we consecrate a fast,
Assemble together in prayer,
And collectively plead before You, O God.
29. Let us remember You on our knees.
Let us recall You when we hunger and thirst
Let us be reminded of You when we come together.

30. For our unification is Your glorification,
Where Your name will be exalted above all else.

31. Your name will remain forever,
And continue throughout the generations;

32. From Abraham to Isaac to Jacob,
Your name will reflect the great I AM;

33. For I AM who I AM is worthy of praise,
Because of the faithful concern for Your people.

34. A concern revealed through an eternal promise
Of the seed, the land, and the blessing.

35. You O God, will not forget Your chosen people,
You are the great I AM.

36. With love and wonder,
O God, maintain a relationship with Your people,

37. As it was yesterday, as it is today, and as it will be forever;
A name worthy of praise!

38. Beyond all imagination and understanding,
The Triune God continues to exist in the invisible and unknown;
Known as God the Father,
The Son,
And the Holy Spirit;
The Three incomprehensible Members intertwine into One.

39. Praise be to the One,
With Your divine nature and wisdom,
All can actively know and experience the throne of restoration;
Who is omniscient and omnipotent in Three!

PRAYER & FASTING
In Pursuit of Focus

As I continued to work on restoring the cabinets in the back parking lot of the complex, I enjoyed a picturesque view of the downtown Dallas skyscrapers. Typically, my mind drifts and wonders how our city would respond to an act of terrorism. With our apartments being near Love Field, and Southwest Airlines jets flying overhead, I can't even fathom the range of emotions the city of New York went through as a result of 9/11. Thankfully, since the 9/11 terrorist act, the Big Apple has been in constant pursuit of restoration. They haven't given up. Restoration hasn't been easy. Slowly but surely the damage to the city is being repaired. New buildings are being constructed where the old ones fell, and more importantly, the confidence of New Yorkers is being reestablished. New life is taking form in New York City. Many wonder, however, even as politicians and contractors work diligently to improve the city's infrastructure, what is being done to maintain a sense of protection for the city? Are they vulnerable to another attack? Statistically, all major cities in the United States have weak points. It is next to impossible to provide 100% security. So what can people do *to ensure the restoration process continues*?

Allow me to suggest something quite simple, yet scripturally profound—*prayer*. Let me reiterate this. Prayer is the answer to the continuation of restoration. How serious will each of you take my suggestion to pray? Do you believe in the power of prayer? One practical way to find out is, when someone asks you to pray for them, what do you do with their request? I was confronted with this very question on Sunday, January 15, 2006, when a good college friend from Kansas City called my wife and me. My friend recently had a dream that she believed the Lord had laid on her heart, and she wanted us to pray for her request. She explained,

> Last night I had the most real, scary, bewildering dream I think I've ever had. Not even necessarily because of its content, but rather because of the weight that has been set upon my spirit as a result. I do not know that I can bear such a responsibility in prayer. Or does it simply stop at prayer? Am I to contact someone or locate a person who has the authority to deal with such an issue?
>
> The dream began as I was sitting bareback on a large, brown horse. We were standing on a sandy shore in front of what looked like a river. The horse began to thunder its way into the water, but I do not remember being afraid. As we entered, normal properties of water did not apply, as we neither floated nor separated, and I could breathe just as if I were on land. I remained on his back as we scaled the ground

> to the bottom of the river. Suddenly, I looked up and horror filled every part of me. In front of me, lying on her right ear was the head of the Statue of Liberty. I began screaming, "No! Not Monday! Not Monday! Not Monday!" It was terrifying. Immediately after this scene, I saw an explosion. I was no longer under water. I simply saw what I knew to be a bridge of some sort as it exploded into flames and smoke. What was weird though was that the main part of the explosion was actually text as opposed to fire and debris. The word, "Holland" was everywhere. It looked as if someone had taken the word "Holland," typed it up millions of times, cut each word into individual pieces of confetti and threw them into the air. That's the best way I can describe it. That was it. That was the dream.[64]

Not your typical prayer request. Yet, because my friend asked if we would pray for the Holland Tunnel, without hesitation, my wife and I went before the Lord in prayer that night. We didn't know anything about the Holland Tunnel. In fact, I even called my brother-in-law, Garth (a federal agent here in Dallas) to confirm that there was such a place. Even with little knowledge, over the course of six months, I would sporadically pray for the Holland Tunnel. Why? Honestly, I couldn't tell you, except that I knew that I had committed myself to pray for the Holland Tunnel. My friend went out on a limb to share her request with Laura and me, and the "least" we could do was pray. Little did we know, along with other people praying, that prayer was the "most" we could do.

On Friday morning, July 7, 2006, as I was surfing the news on CNN.com, I came across the front-page headline, "N.Y. tunnel plot uncovered."[65] Should I be shocked? Should I be excited? According to the *New York Daily News*, "The plotters wanted to detonate a massive amount of explosives inside the Holland Tunnel to blast a hole that would destroy the tunnel, everyone in it, and send a devastating flood shooting through the streets of lower Manhattan."[66]

God is willing to listen to our prayers. Even when we don't see the answers immediately, or announced on the internet, we must be committed to praying for the continuation of restoration, not only in our lives, but also in our towns, cities, and our nation.

APPROACH

With the recognition of our sinfulness, we simply need to come before Him on our knees in prayer and ask for the Spirit of God to guide and preserve what we begin to restore. Respected author and theologian Robert E. Coleman wrote, "When the channel is clean, the Spirit of God can flow through the believing heart in true intercessory prayer. Such prayer is wrought from hearts overwhelmed with the sense of unworthiness yet captivated by the knowledge of God."[67]

Prayer results from a personal understanding of who man has become, and a deeper longing for who God was, is, and will always be. Thankfully, the Lord is willing to love us unconditionally and grant us an eternal relationship with Him through faith alone in Jesus Christ. Even though we are saved through justification, we must recognize our spiritual condition and return to Him on a daily basis. In speaking to the people of Israel, the prophet Joel revealed the Lord's desire for us to come before Him when he wrote, "'Yet even now,' declares the Lord, 'Return to Me with all your heart, and with fasting, weeping and mourning; and rend your heart and not your garments.'"[68] The Lord is providing an opportunity for His people to come before Him for "repentance, remorse and renewal."[69] It is a matter of *focus*. God is willing and ready to listen and answer. But it is our decision to tap into the Divine phone line which is open twenty-four hours with no busy signal.

Are we ready to approach God with everything we have? Are we ready to turn to the Lord in prayer? Are we prepared to focus on our relationship with the Lord through fasting? Do we hurt to the point of weeping for our own current spiritual condition? Do we mourn over the present state of our relationship with the Lord? As in the days of the prophet Joel, I am not talking about tearing one's clothing to express grief and remorse. Returning to the Lord doesn't begin with an outward action[70] because, for all we know, the actions are not sincere. Rather, to return to the Lord must begin with a heart condition that only each person can change. It can only come from personal analysis and no one else.

I found this to be 100% true for myself. No one could tell me I needed to seek the Lord, and then assume it would happen. If I wanted to experience change, I needed to do it myself. At the same time, I needed the Lord's guidance. So, during my senior year in college, I decided to come before the Lord with consistent prayer. I wanted to show my complete commitment to the Lord. Each and every morning, before I would begin the day serving and selling coffee at The Jumping Bean (located on campus), I would go into the closet where I stored all of the coffee shop supplies and equipment, and I would pray. I would ask God for direction. I would ask that whatever I do, He be glorified. I just wanted God to move in my life. I wanted Him to reveal

Himself to me, and I must say, I wasn't prepared for His powerful answer. It would become a defining event in my life, a real "Damascus Road" experience.

One evening, as I was washing dishes at midnight, a customer came and began talking to me. She asked one question, "What do you want to do with your life?" I remember responding without hesitation, "I just want to lead and train others in their relationship with God." Though I did not know, specifically, what my goals entailed, I felt convicted that this was the direction the Lord wanted me to go.

Immediately, this customer asked if she could lie down on the couch (in the student union) and close her eyes before the Lord. Why not? What did I have to lose? At this time, I really didn't know this girl except through serving her drinks at the coffee shop, but if someone wanted to pray for me, then by all means. So, for the next forty-five minutes, she lied on the blue couch in the student union. She didn't say anything aloud. She kept to herself. What was I to do? At one point, campus safety came and asked if everything was okay. Since I was the owner of the coffee shop, I assured them everything was fine. In my mind, I was a little confused and a little excited. So not knowing how to respond, I too prayed.

Then, around 1:00 a.m., a student came running to the union, where he pounded on the outside door. Startled, I went over and asked if there was something he needed. He explained that he had been over at the prayer chapel and felt led to come over to the union and pray for me. I glanced over at the customer, who was still lying down on the couch, and then I looked at college student. I shrugged my shoulders, and said, "By all means, come on in."

Here it was, early in the morning, and two somewhat "unknown" individuals were praying for me. Unaware of how real and present the Lord was at the time, I continued to pray. What was going on? I could only entrust this situation to the Lord, and pray that He be glorified according to Scripture.

The customer finally came to, and sat up. The college student then lifted his head and came over to us. We talked a bit about how the Lord was revealing Himself at this hour and decided I should remain downstairs, praying alone. At the same time, both individuals headed upstairs to the second floor of the student union. When I was done praying, with my sandals kicked off at the foot of the stairs and my dish towel in hand, I went upstairs where both college students were waiting to pray for me.

In those early morning hours of April 6, 2001, on the second floor of the student union at Taylor University, the God of Abraham, Isaac, and Jacob faithfully revealed Himself to me. With all of my sinfulness, my pride and my lust set before the Lord, I believe the sovereign Lord called me to follow Him. I mustn't be afraid of what lies ahead. I mustn't doubt the direction. I must confidently be devoted to pursuing the path He has promised for my life and, with a commitment to the truth and Spirit, the Lord will continue to remain true to His word to me.

I can't imagine how I would know the direction of my life, if I wasn't committed to prayer. Because of my desire to hear from God for guidance, I was committed to the power of prayer. No matter the response. Regardless of what I had done in the past, God is still willing to listen. This is exactly what the prophet Joel said to his fellow countrymen. He encouraged the Israelites not to worry about how God would respond to personal restoration, when he wrote, "Now return to the Lord your God, for He is gracious and compassionate, slow to anger, abounding in lovingkindness and relenting of evil. Who knows whether He will not turn and relent and leave a blessing behind Him, even a grain offering and a drink offering for the Lord your God?"[71]

ACTIVE

We are at a point in time when we, as believers, are ready for a basic yet authentic change here in the United States of America. The church in America is like those kitchen cabinets, with scars and stains all too long neglected. We need to pray for restoration. We need to cry aloud, "Stir up Your power and come to save us! O God, restore us and cause Your face to shine upon us, and we will be saved."[72] There will be no change unless we pray for it. God is waiting to respond to our requests. We need to pray for a renewed closeness to the Lord by the power of the Holy Spirit.[73] With this kind of prayer, we can collectively begin to worship the Lord in truth and spirit.[74]

The prophet Joel made it known to the people of Israel that they must return to the Lord, both personally and collectively, as a unified body. In order to experience restoration in the nation of Israel, Joel commanded his peers:

> Blow a trumpet in Zion,
> Consecrate a fast, proclaim a solemn assembly,
> Gather the people, sanctify the congregation,
> Assemble the elders,
> Gather the children and the nursing infants.
> Let the bridegroom come out of his room
> And the bride out of her bridal chamber.[75]

Restoration *must* be a collective effort, and there is no time to delay. Joel called the entire worshipping community together and no one was excluded.[76] Even newlyweds, who were typically excused from their daily prayers on the day of the wedding, were not exempt from attending this unique and special call for prayer and fasting. A spiritual emergency was at hand.[77] Dr. Thomas Constable restated the importance of this gathering when he wrote, "God's people needed to gather together and re-consecrate themselves to Him as a people."[78]

Nothing on a nationwide scale, for the body of Christ, has happened in the twenty-first century. Why? Could it be that the body of Christ in America has lacked in unified prayer and fasting? God is working mightily in the lives of His people on a daily basis, yet Americans have not seen any major movement of renewal and restoration.

We need to blow the trumpet and grab the *focus* of the followers of Jesus Christ. What does this fine-tuned focus look like? Allow me to first suggest that we need to refocus on a lost discipline—*fasting*. Fasting is a foreign word to most within the church in America, but this discipline is as biblical as prayer and reading Scripture. It implies that we set aside a specific item, such as food, water, television, internet, radio, shopping, etc., in order to intentionally turn to the Lord. We need to sacrificially and voluntarily do something to rid ourselves of all the things that take our attention away from God. Because currently, too many "things" in our culture today interfere with our much-needed hunger for God.[79] As John Piper said:

> If you don't feel strong desires for the manifestation of the glory of God, it is not because you have drunk deeply and are satisfied.

> It is because you have nibbled so long at the table of the world. You soul is stuffed with small things, and there is no room for the great. God did not create you for this. There is an appetite for God. And it can be awakened. I invite you to turn from the dulling effects of food and the dangers of idolatry, and to say with some simple fast: "This much, O God, I want you."[80]

Fasting is a discipline we must choose to participate in. Do we want more of God? According to the Gospel of Matthew, Jesus referenced that His followers would fast. He said, "But the days will come when the bridegroom (Jesus) is taken away from them, and then they will fast."[81] *(parentheses refer to author input)* Why will the followers of Jesus fast? We will fast because we are to long for something more—Jesus.

Through the discipline of fasting, the church in America can look to further the process of revival. We must, however, understand that fasting is not a quick way to get God's attention; rather it allows us to be more sensitive to what the Lord wants. Edith Schaeffer, a twentieth-century writer commented:

> Is fasting ever a bribe to get God to pay more attention to the petitions? No, a thousand times no. It is simply a way to make clear that we sufficiently reverence the amazing opportunity to ask help from the everlasting God, the Creator of the universe, to choose to put everything else aside and concentrate on worshiping, asking for forgiveness, and making our requests

> known—considering His help more important than anything we could do ourselves in our own strength and with our own ideas.[82]

Aside from fasting, prayer is *the* essential thing that we can do to bring about a restoration in this country. Joel wrote:

> Let the priests, the Lord's ministers,
> Weep between the porch and the altar,
> And let them say, "Spare Your people, O Lord,
> And do not make Your inheritance a reproach,
> A byword among the nations.
> Why should they among the peoples say,
> 'Where is their God?' "[83]

According to this Old Testament, the priests were to be the ones who spearheaded this time of prayer. But now, because of our relationship with Jesus Christ, we have become the royal priesthood. Simon Peter wrote, "But you are a chosen race, a royal priesthood, a holy nation, a people for God's own possession, so that you may proclaim the excellencies of Him who has you out of darkness into His marvelous light; for you were not a people, but now you are the people of God; you had not received mercy, but now you have received mercy."[84] We all must pray. Businessmen, bums, black men, white women, Hispanic kids, pastors, teachers, missionaries, criminals ... heck, even maintenance men! With faith in Christ, we can all come to the Lord on equal ground. Samuel Chadwick referred to the prayer of man when he said:

> There is no power like that of prevailing prayer—of Abraham pleading for Sodom, Jacob wrestling in the stillness of the night, Moses standing in the breach, Hannah intoxicated with sorrow, David heartbroken with remorse and grief, Jesus in sweat of blood. Add to this list from the records of the church your personal observation and experience, and always there is the cost of passion unto blood. Such prayer prevails. It turns ordinary mortals into men of power. It brings power. It brings fire. It brings rain. It brings life. It brings God.[85]

God is preparing the hearts and minds of all believers across this country to experience a time of awakening through prayer. Even if we recognize that we need the Lord, restoration will only occur when prayer is given the appropriate respect. Former professor of Spurgeon's College in London, Lewis Drummond wrote, "I have become absolutely convinced that lack of prayer is the only reason revival has not yet come in our day. Unless we add that leaven in our spiritual lump, the recipe for revival is ruined and the bread for the hungry will never rise."[86]

Throughout Scripture, men and women understood the importance of prayer. Their prayers faithfully expected mighty answers from the Lord. They believed the Lord would shower down His blessings upon them. Over the course of the Old Testament, specifically to the prophets, God confirmed to His people that would respond to them. Isaiah recorded the words of God:

> For I will pour out water on the thirsty land
> And streams on the dry ground;

> I will pour out My Spirit on your offspring
> And My blessing on your descendants.[87]

God is willing to save them and restore His people. Yet, in today's society, we limit our prayers. We ask with doubt, rather than with faith. E.M. Bounds said:

> We are ever ready to excuse our lack of earnest and toilsome praying.... We often end praying just where we ought to begin. We quit praying when God.... is waiting for us to really pray. We are deterred by obstacles from praying as we submit to difficulties and call it submission to God's will.[88]

Wouldn't it be great to witness a Spirit-led revival down as a response to prayer? I urge each of us to unite as the body of Christ and pray for such a feat. In order to pray, we don't need to be from the same denomination, town or state. We just need to be like-minded in prayer for revival. David's son, Solomon, prayed for the people of Israel, and in response, God promised the Israelites' requests would be answered. The Almighty God said, "And My people who are called by My name humble themselves and pray and seek My face and turn from their wicked ways, then I will hear from heaven, will forgive their sin and will heal their land."[89]

My friends, just as the kitchen cabinets were restored in apartment #215, so can our lives with the Lord be restored. It all begins with our willingness to acknowledge that it is time for a change—for *restoration*—and there is no better time than now. There are no short cuts. It will not happen overnight. We must be steadfast in our desire and our commitment—a personal commitment to confession and prayer. We must be willing to rid ourselves of sin in order to draw near to the Lord. With a clear conscience, we can approach God on our knees praying for personal change, and a nationwide movement towards restoration.

I write these words from personal experience. During the last semester of my senior year at Taylor University, the Lord was moving in my life. I saw it firsthand in my prayer life. Yet, I wanted to hear more of how the Lord was moving, specifically in the lives of others. So I began to collectively pray with others for change on our college campus.

Initially, I asked a friend from Chicago, to pray with me about the spiritual condition of Taylor. So, in the small coffee room, the two of us prayed. The next day I asked my roommate from Nebraska to join us. For a couple of days, it was just us three amigos praying for Taylor. We didn't know what the results would be. We didn't know how we would see the Lord respond to our prayers. We just wanted to see the Spirit move on our campus. We wanted the complacency to come to a halt. We wanted for all of the student body to taste and experience the Lord firsthand. We wanted others to live for Jesus and we believed the results would come through the power of prayer.

During these days, I organized a time of sharing testimonies at my coffee shop called "Conversations at the Bean." This entailed each dorm "wing" (a small informal version of a fraternity or sorority) on campus to come and have two to three individuals share how they came to know Jesus Christ as their Savior and how He was currently impacting their lives. Sometimes five people showed up, sometimes it was thirty-five. No matter the number, before the wing would arrive, the three of us would get together and pray for those individuals. Slowly but surely more people began to come and pray with us. We didn't promote it. We didn't advertise it. People just began to show up. Eventually we had to leave the coffee closet room, and head upstairs. Three people turned into fifteen. All we were doing was praying. No agenda. No schedule. It was just prayer before the Lord as the body of Christ. A true kindred spirit began to form amongst the people of prayer.

One day, a motivated student came to the coffee shop early in the morning and asked me about the unique pulse on campus. He noticed something was going on, and wanted to know what role he could play. I told him that a few people were praying for the Spirit to move on Taylor's campus. I also mentioned that others were coming to share their testimony in front of their peers. Other than that, I said all we desire is for believers to be more intentional about their relationship with Jesus. He smiled, said thanks, and left the coffee counter.

Normally, because of my coffee shop responsibilities, I was not able to go to any of the daily chapels on campus, but I felt the Lord leading me to attend. So, I quickly closed the shop, and headed over to catch the benediction from the campus pastor. I missed it, but as students, faculty and staff were headed out of chapel the student from the coffee shop hopped up onto the stage. He asked for everyone to come back. Chapel was not over.

Before the entire study body, he confessed his complacency with the Lord, and challenged others to get right with Him. Immediately, an outpouring of the Spirit occurred. Hundreds of individuals from all over the chapel flooded the stage. More people came to the front and got on their knees. Others grabbed the microphone and confessed their sins. I could not believe what I was witnessing, yet I felt no surprise, no shock. The Lord was moving on our campus and He was responding to our prayers. In fact, later that night at our usual prayer time, what started as three people in a coffee house closet grew to more than 250 people! We had to meet outside to pray that night. The Lord was moving on our campus—it was because the power of prayer was being utilized by the body of Christ.

ENGAGE

Let each of us ask this question of ourselves: Do we engage in continuous prayer? Is something so heavy on our heart that we will "pray without ceasing"?[90] My proposal is that we pray fervently for revival. But we need to be committed to coming before God in prayer for this massive request. If we keep on asking, we will receive. If we keep on seeking, we will find. If we keep on knocking, the door will be opened. Jesus taught His disciples about this persevering power of prayer:

> Ask, and it will be given to you; seek, and you will find; knock, and it will be opened to you. For everyone who asks receives, and he who seeks finds, and to him who knocks it will be opened. Or what man is there among you who, when his son asks for a loaf, will give him a stone? Or if he asks for a fish, he will not give him a snake, will he? If you then, being evil, know how to give good gifts to your children, how much more will your Father who is in heaven give what is good to those who ask Him![91]

So, when we pray, do we pray with expectation? Do we expect the Lord to move as a result of our prayers? God is waiting to lavishly pour Himself upon His people, but we need to have the mindset of expectation in our prayer life. We are to "believe that (we) have already received whatever (we) request in prayer."[92] *(parentheses refer to author input)* Jesus Christ said:

> Have faith in God. Truly I say to you, whoever says to his mountain, "Be taken up and cast into the sea," and does not doubt in his heart, but believes that what he says is going to happen, it will be granted him. Therefore I say to you, all things for which you pray and ask, believe that you have received them, and they will be granted you.[93]

According to H. Wayne House, "The blessings and provisions of God are available to every one of His children."[94] God delights in giving good gifts to each one of us "who persist in prayer."[95] So how can this be possible? As mere humans, can we really approach God in prayer and know that He will listen? By what means do we have to come before God? The answer to all these questions is Jesus Christ. Jesus Himself told His disciples that He will take our prayer requests to God the Father. He is the means of our prayers. Jesus said:

> Truly, truly, I say to you, he who believes in Me, the works that I do, he will do also; and greater works than these he will do; because I go to the Father. Whatever you ask in My name, that will I do, so that the Father may be glorified in the Son. If you ask Me anything in My name, I will do it.[96]

Jesus will respond to our prayers. Now, please don't read this section and think that I am promoting prayers for personal health and wealth, a concept known as "prosperity theology." In each of the above New Testament passages, Jesus Christ is speaking to His disciples. These passages were essential to provide comfort for these disciples. Times were unclear and uncertain, and the disciples were reassured that they would be taken care of by God. The disciples were taught to have faith that they could trust God with any and all of their requests. They needed to believe, with or without Christ being physically present on earth, that they could approach God with their prayer concerns and requests. And, just as these profound words from Christ were meant for the first-century apostles, they were also meant for the current church in America. Like the disciples, we need to be assured that we can place our trust in God through faith. When we communicate with the Lord, we need to have the confidence that God will hear us and respond to our needs. However, nowhere in these passages did Christ intend for the audience to abuse this asking-receiving relationship between God and His people for personal gain and satisfaction. Rather, with our trust in God, we can confidently be assured that He will respond to our needs, and never leave us nor forsake us.

How should we pray then? While giving His most famous sermon, Jesus Christ gave the perfect example when explaining prayer to His disciples. He said:

> Pray, then in this way: "Our Father who is in heaven, hallowed be Your name. Your kingdom come. Your will be done, on earth as it is in heaven. Give us this day our daily bread. And forgive us our debts, as we also have forgiven our

> debtors. And do not lead us into temptation, but deliver us from evil. For Yours is the kingdom and the power and the glory forever. Amen."[97]

Based on these helpful and insightful words of Jesus Christ, three principles take form in my own prayer life. They are:

Prayer Principle #1

> Pray to the Sovereign God with an expectant faith that asks Him to make His will known here on earth as it is in heaven.

Prayer Principle #2

> Pray to God that He will bring glory to His name in all things.

Prayer Principle #3

> Pray to the Father in Heaven and ask Him to provide the daily essentials needed in life.

Restoration to the body in Christ in America can occur when we are committed to prayer as a collective body. Like the prophet Joel when he approached the Israelites, I, too now come before the believers of Jesus Christ, and ask each one of you to a disciplined structure of prayer. This organized gathering will not only benefit the local denominations, but also the cities and states we reside in. The Lord is ready and waiting to pour His blessings upon His people, *but we must ask Him*, while keeping in mind the prayer principles outlined by Christ in the Sermon on the Mount. When the people of Israel returned to the Lord in a unified manner in the time of Joel, the Lord responded. God promised deliverance to the nation of Israel when Joel wrote:

> Then the Lord will be zealous for His land and will have pity on His people. The Lord will answer and say to this people, "Behold, I am going to send you grain, new wine and oil, and you will be satisfied in full with them; and I will never again make you a reproach among the nations...
>
> Do not fear, O land, rejoice and be glad, for the Lord has done great things."
>
> ... So rejoice, O sons of Zion, and be glad in the Lord your God; for He has given you the early rain for your vindication. And He has poured down for you the rain, the early and latter rain as before. The threshing floors will be full of grain, and the vats will overflow with the new wine and oil...
>
> You will have plenty to eat and be satisfied and praise the name of the Lord your God who has dealt wondrously with you; then My people will never be put to shame.[98]

It seems impossible. It looks like darkness will engulf the light here in America. But, to the contrary, the Lord desires to work wonders through the local denominations, and collectively impact others all throughout America. The Lord wants to respond to His people. However, we will never know and experience this restoration, unless we gather together in assembly before the Lord.

When we actually follow through with this pursuit of collectively coming together in prayer and fasting, do we believe God will answer? (Remember the Holland Tunnel dream?) The answer is spelled out clearly, according to the prophet Joel:

> It will come about after this *(the assembly of His people)*
> That I will pour out My Spirit on all mankind;
> And your sons and daughters will prophesy,
> Your old men will dream dreams,
> Your young men will see visions.
> Even on the male and female servants
> I will pour out My Spirit in those days.[99]
> *(parentheses refer to author input)*

The time is now. We mustn't delay any longer. We are in a spiritual crisis, and we must call upon the Lord for restoration. When we do, the Spirit will pour upon the body of Christ in America like we have never seen before.

EXTRAORDINARY RESULTS

The process of returning to the Lord on a daily basis has not come naturally to me. I am a true American. A firecracker by birth, I was born on the Fourth of July ready to explode with independence. Even though the Pledge of Allegiance included "One nation, under God," my destination did not necessarily include the Lord. It included only me. As I gazed upon Old Glory and said the pledge, I focused on one star (my star of allegiance), and pledged allegiance not only to my country but to my successful future. Growing up in small-town Indiana, I proudly pursued my star of allegiance. I was determined to leave a stripe of history, a stripe that others might admire and wish to emulate. The beating of my inner drum was patriotic—liberty and justice for all. The path I pursued was red, white and blue. I was living the American dream. But, unlike the Pledge of Allegiance, I was not really living "under God." I didn't recognize Him often; rather I relied on myself because the emphasis was on me. What was best for me? What did I want? I was a believer. I went to church. I read my Bible and I even prayed, but something was missing. God was a concept to me, but not a reality.[100] I didn't put complete *faith* in Him when it came to making personal decisions. I placed all *hope* in my professional career. I shared *love* with others, but only as a tool to selfishly gain something for myself. I was taught that the Lord desired to know and experience Him intimately but, no doubt about it, I was not listening. There finally came a point when I knew I could no longer run from the Lord.

> *I needed to be restored by Him in order to be near to Him.*

No one but me could initiate this restoration. Not my pastor, not my parents, not my college buddies from Taylor University. Only I could change my desire for personal restoration in my life. I needed to draw near to God by letting myself go. Just as I recognized my need for personal restoration, as a believer, I believe restoration is also knocking on the front door of the church in America. I pray this gentle knock will soon develop into a thundering bang. A change can only occur if we are committed to opening the door and walking through it in pursuit of holiness and a divine response. We each have to find our own desire to know and experience the Lord and we have to ask the Lord, in prayer, to help us accomplish this restoration task. Restoration is a process, and life has much more to offer, for those who seek it.

A SERVANT'S REQUEST

Being *extraordinary* through holiness

40. The outcome of restoration remains unwritten;
Thus, let us grow as people of transformation set aside for Your glory.

41. A heavenly glory revealed through our human deed,
To become a city on a hill
And a lamp on a stand.

42. We proclaim Your name O God,
For Your grace and mercy
Bleeds eternally through Your Son Jesus Christ;
Where justification is established,
Holiness is required,
And glorification is promised.

43. But O God,
Allow us to recall, the power of the Spirit has been received,
And as witnesses,
We have been commissioned;
No longer must we ignore the fulfillment of the law.

44. Rather let us keep what we know to be true,
And remember the instructions;

45. O God, we are to be baptizing and teaching others,
Just as Your Son would have us do.

46. Thankfully, You will never leave nor forsake us,
For any who believe in the Almighty,
Guidance will come from the Helper;
Where love is obvious,
Joy and peace are apparent,
Patience and kindness are revealed,
Goodness and faithfulness are evident,
Gentleness is displayed,
And self-control is confidently manifested.

HOLINESS

In Pursuit of Being Extraordinary

I always survey Swissaire Apartments with the eyes of a maintenance man. Consciously, I form a checklist in my head for projects I will be doing that week. Whatever the task will be, the work mustn't be avoided. I could shy away from physical labor and effort to be put forward, but then improvements, progress, and updates would never get done. It would still look and feel like the 1950s.

One thing is for sure, we have a parking lot that provides a good sense of security. It resembles a prison compound with a seven foot fence and sharp razor wire around the top. The rear entrance has its individual punch code on the door, the laundry room facility (located in the rear) has the same key code security. Why? Because the area of the city in which we live is rough. Homeless roam our streets late at night. Alcoholics and drug addicts frequent the area in the early morning. Nationally, Dallas has the highest crime per capita for a city over one million in the United States (as of 2006). The most common crime in our area is car theft. So, with massive halogen floods pouring their light out over razor-wire fence, Swissaire trics to protect the tenant's vehicles parked within its' fence.

With the constant flow of vehicles driving and parking in the limited space behind the apartments, I notice the parking lot is in need of some new repair. *But where would I start?* Without a sense of direction, I knew I would feel overwhelmed. So, with so much work to be done, I created a prioritized list in my head. The first year, I decided to replace the torn and battered exit driveway with new concrete. Why? Because tenants would literally have to dodge a two-foot drop off as they drove out. By the second year, it was time to repaint and brighten the yellow of the direction arrows and lines of the parking spaces. It was also time to replace the individual signs over each tenant's parking space. This involved cutting and engraving individual each sign from natural pieces of wood. In the third year, I noticed the parking lot poles were rusting away and in desperate need of repair. So, with lots of elbow grease, primer and paint, the poles again looked new. I also had to replace the garbage dumpster, which then led to replacing the railing on the stairs to the garbage dumpster. My most recent project was painting the driveway curb. With an entrance driveway of eight feet wide and an exit driveway of nine feet wide, the curbing was constantly being abused. So, in an effort to caution the tenants as they hurry in and scurry out, I got on my knees for a week and hand-rolled "safety-yellow" paint along 280 feet of curbing. In a weird way, the newly painted curb makes the subtle statement "slow down" while, at the same time, screams "beware of the narrow surroundings!"

You see, progress toward improvement is only made when the effort is put forth. When the work is done, the proof will be evident to others. The progress will take time. Just as the parking lot is in constant need of upkeep we, too, must realize that we need to live and maintain a refreshing, new lifestyle of holiness. As confirmed in the Epistle written to the Ephesians, Christ's love was given in order for our lives to be made holy from the beginning of our creation. The apostle Paul wrote, "Long before He laid down the earth's foundation, he had us in mind, had settled on us as the focus of his love, to be made whole and holy by his love."[101]

Many Americans ask, "Does God really have a plan for America?" One thing is for sure, God does have a plan and purpose for *the body of Christ* within America. Because of the love of Jesus in our lives, we are to live a holy life. As members of the body of Christ, we are to be "set apart" from our neighbors. As followers of Jesus, we are to be "set apart" from other religions. To live as Jesus lived requires a lifestyle of holiness. We must ask ourselves, as Christians, are we willing to spend the time and expend the energy required to pursue holiness in our lives? Do we really want to be different? Do we really want to be distinct? If the answer is yes to any of the above, we must allow holiness—the daily outcome of our faith in Jesus Christ—to begin to reveal itself, in an unconditional manner, where we serve Jesus with all of our heart, soul, and mind.

IDENTIFY

It is important to understand how holiness begins. Holiness, also known as sanctification, begins with God. Theologically, "It is most important for us to realize that sanctification (holiness) is not something that we do by ourselves, with our own efforts and in our own strength. Sanctification is not a human activity, but a divine gift."[102] When we understand and accept this divine gift, sanctification (holiness) will instantly occur. This gift of God, according to Baker's Dictionary of Theology is, "Jesus Christ, and Jesus Christ means grace. He is the grace of God towards us."[103] Jesus made the ultimate sacrifice, by dying for our sins, so that we may receive the free gift of eternal life. Through this undeserved gift, we are justified by faith in Jesus Christ. This gift of grace is neither deserved, nor earned. When we have a humble heart, we become grateful and understand the magnitude of the crucifixion. The fact is, we have all sinned and fallen short of His glory. Thankfully, Christ died so that we may be saved and granted a relationship with Him forever and ever.

God's grace allows our lives to be free of shame and guilt. Even though we may feel unworthy of God's love and attention, as Simon Peter did when he fell at the feet of Jesus,[104] we can still live in freedom because of the new life we have in Christ. It is only through faith in Christ and His gift of grace that we are justified. With the power of the Holy Spirit, we are able to step closer to the Lord our God and experience the journey of holiness.

To experience holiness, our eternal focus must be restored.[105] We are to fix our eyes "not on what is seen, but on what is unseen."[106] We know and trust that Christ is seated in a place of divine authority. As the King of all kings, Jesus has victoriously overcome our daily struggles against the world, the flesh, and Satan. But do we, as the body of Christ in America, believe this? The apostle Paul wrote to the Colossians, "Therefore if you have been raised up with Christ, keep seeking the things above, where Christ is, seated at the right hand of God. Set your mind on the things above, not on the things that are on earth."[107]

If we choose to follow Jesus Christ, then our lives should become living evidence for the Lord if we are centered on the ascended and glorified Christ seated at the right hand of the Father. One theologian has the right perspective: "The Christian has to keep his feet upon the earth, but his head in the heavens. He must be heavenly-minded here on earth and so help to make earth like heaven."[108] We take up a unique role as followers of the Lord. We live here on earth as aliens and strangers. Where Christ resides is where we desire to be. Earth is not our home, heaven is.

Life is too short to focus on short-lived goals that have little or no eternal value. The irony of this invaluable life lesson wasn't learned the first-time around that I lived in Dallas or even the second time I lived here. It wasn't until eight years later, after the Lord brought me back to Dallas for a third time that I learned the importance of holiness. Just like progress on the parking lot, my personal change and growth occurred over a long period of time.

For the first go around in Dallas, I was a sophomore in college when I decided to pursue the personal dream of being more integrated in the professional sports industry. I had recently finished an internship with a Continental Basketball Association (CBA) team, the Fort Wayne Fury in Indiana, and I wanted to move up the ladder in the sports profession. I believed it was time to get more exposure to the sports world, and more connections within. Precisely why I decided to work for Hoop-It-Up, which at the time was "the official 3-on-3 basketball tour of the NBA and NBC Sports,"[109] a company located in Dallas. My job was to travel the west-coast setting up basketball tournaments, while personally establishing contacts within the NBA and NBC.

The second summer in Dallas, I worked as an intern for The Marketing Arm (TMA), which at the time was solely a sports marketing agency that created and negotiated deals between professional athletes and corporations. To give you a better visual, this company was like the sports marketing version of *Jerry McGuire.* The company was to "show the money" to the athletes. In one summer, my role within the company was to specifically develop case studies for either potential or current client-athletes.

This internship then led to working the 2000 Sugar Bowl, which was the NCAA National Championship game located in New Orleans. Needless to say, it was quite the experience. To interact with ESPN, the college teams from Florida State and Virginia Tech, employees with NOKIA, former and current NFL players, and other celebrities was a selfish-rush. I loved every minute of it. But it was all about me. How could I further my career in the sports industry?

One thing is for sure, I absolutely loved the company that I was working for. The Marketing Arm was a great company, and I couldn't say enough good things about how they operated as a company, and how they took care of their clients. In fact, I met with the current owner and we talked about future possibilities with the company upon my college graduation. Things were looking good for the future—the future of the current and temporary world.

Thankfully, the Lord revealed to me that I needed to change my perspective. I needed to put on the glasses of eternity and, through the means of Laura, my wife (who was my girlfriend at the time) I was able to do so. Pride had become thick to the point where I couldn't see anyone else around me. I couldn't think of anything except myself. God had dropped on my life's list of priorities. Things needed to change, because I was traveling down the road of temporary happiness, the one that eventually leads to nowhere. As the late revivalist Dr. Vance Havner said:

> God didn't save you to make you happy. That's a by-product. He saved you to make you holy. You were predestined to be conformed to the image of God's Son.[110]

After being in Dallas for a couple of summers, the choices I made looked good in the public eye, but in all reality, I had chosen the easy and wide path. A path lined with possible personal fortune and fame. I knew it was time to change. This would be a process, but I needed to refocus my steps and head down a different path. It was time to set my sights on the less-traveled path, the narrow path, the path of holiness. I wanted to follow in the footsteps of Jesus. Please don't hear me say that the pursuit of holiness isn't possible in the sports industry. For myself, though, I needed to escape from the tempting environment of pride and grow in the Lord. I was lacking in spiritual maturity.

After graduating from Taylor University, Laura and I got married. We moved to Nashville, Tennessee, for one year and then the Lord brought me back to Dallas, this time with a new focus. I wasn't going to be pursuing the wide path I had discovered in the sports world, rather, I was going to be studying the Bible at the Dallas Theological Seminary, which was just down the street from the offices of The Marketing Arm.

What an ironic God! Instead of being consumed with myself and my career, my perspective changed. Christ was to be my focus. I was done announcing my personal achievements. My life would be all about Christ. As John the Baptist stated, "He (Jesus) must increase, but I must decrease *(parentheses refer to author input)* How is this possible, after a lifelong pursuit of selfishness? How did I plan to keep my eyes on Christ and pursue holiness? The answer is quite simple—I would invest my time in the Word of God. Like the apostle James wrote, I had become "like a newborn baby longing for the pure milk of the word, so that by it (I) may grow in respect to salvation."[111] I knew I needed to be intentional about studying the Scriptures, in a disciplined environment, where I could grow in the Word of God. It was exactly what I needed. Seminary might not be for everyone, but I needed it. The Lord knew it, and He brought me back to Dallas. My perspective on life slowly began to change from the temporary to the eternal. Time is too short not to invest, whole-heartedly, into the kingdom of God.

We do not know how long we will physically live on earth. In the book of James, he wrote, "Yet you do not know what your life will be like tomorrow. You are just a vapor that appears for a little while and then vanishes away."[112] Life will come and go. We will vanish from this earth, but we have an eternal future with Christ. We are not guaranteed the future, so we must live in the present. We cannot sit back and twiddle our thumbs of faith. Paul understood that Jesus Christ must be our focus. The apostle Paul confirmed this mentality when he wrote, "For you have died and your life is hidden with Christ in God."[113] Jesus Christ should be all that we know. Jesus Christ should be all that we understand. Jesus Christ should be our life. Why does Paul emphasize this to the Colossian Church? Because there are eternal results for an undivided attention devoted to Him.

Paul continued, "When Christ, who is our life, is revealed, then you also will be revealed with Him in glory."[114] Not only will we spend eternity with Him, but we will join Christ in the clouds when He returns for His people. The Lord will be glorified! What a joy to think about! The author Norman Geisler summarized Paul's thoughts about refocusing our thoughts on Christ, "So Paul added a new direction to the believers' focus of attention: they should look upward to Christ's reign over them in heaven and also forward to His return for them in the clouds."[115] The time is now.

RELY

Holiness begins with our focus on Jesus. It continues to flourish when we *turn away from the unholy behavior that is quickly becoming the way of today's world.* We are to pursue sanctification and *ignore the desires of the flesh.* Holiness requires us to be different and distinct; it requires that we not proceed with lives of sin. The world-renowned theologian John R.W. Stott addressed this very issue of sin in a Christian's life when he said, "The Christian life begins with a death to sin. And in view of this it is ridiculous to ask if we are at liberty to continue in sin. How can we go on living in what we have died to?"[116] Our lives must be evidence of what we believe. The apostle Paul called upon the believers to exemplify this commitment to the Lord. He knew that growth would only occur when we rid ourselves of our past lifestyle. The key to moving forward in holiness is to not give into the sins of our past. In other words, my pride must be kicked to the curb. Author Eugene Peterson interpreted Paul's words beautifully in *The Message*:

> And that means killing off everything connected with that way of death: sexual promiscuity, impurity, lust, doing whatever you feel like whenever you feel like it, and grabbing whatever attracts your fancy. That's a life shaped by things and feelings instead of by God. It's because of this kind of thing that God is about to explode in anger. It wasn't long ago that you were doing

> all that stuff and not knowing any better. But you know better now, so make sure it's all gone for good: bad temper, irritability, meanness, profanity, dirty talk.[117]

The fact of the matter is, once we decide to follow Christ, we commit ourselves to "walk in a manner worthy of the calling with which (we) have been called."[118] *(parentheses refer to author input)* We must no longer walk in the steps of the past that lead to our sinful lifestyle. A past that displayed a lifestyle darkened by our ignorance in which we walked with our hearts hardened and our skin thick and calloused. We looked to "practice every kind of impurity with greediness"[119] and self-gratification had become our personal focus. This must stop because we "did not learn Christ in this way."[120]

As believers, *if* we are ready and willing, we must strip ourselves of the dirt and filth we were once clothed in, and reveal that Christ has cleansed and changed our lives forever. Again, Eugene Peterson's modern language of the book of Colossians says:

> Don't lie to one another. You're done with that old life. It's like a filthy set of ill-fitting clothes you've stripped off and put in the fire. Now you're dressed in a new wardrobe. Every item of your new way of life is custom-made by the Creator, with his label on it. All the old fashions are obsolete. Words like Jewish and non-Jewish, religious and irreligious, insider and outsider, uncivilized and uncouth, slave and free, mean nothing. From now on everyone is defined by Christ, everyone is included in Christ.[121]

If the body of Christ in America is ready and willing, this will happen. Why do I say if?

Because holiness will *only* occur:

If we understand who we are in Jesus

If we really live for Him

If we receive the ways of Jesus, and

If we believe Jesus is the truth.[122]

If we grasp who Jesus Christ is in our personal lives, we will set aside who we were before we placed our trust in Jesus Christ. Or, as Paul wrote, we will "lay aside the old self, which is being corrupted in accordance with the lusts of deceit."[123] Each of us has become a "new man" in Christ Jesus. This phrase, *new man*, doesn't imply that we have become reincarnated, only that the nature of our person is newly-found, with different and distinct qualities. We are not living for ourselves, but for Jesus Christ. When Paul wrote to the church at Corinth, he reminded them of their identity in Christ, "Therefore if anyone is in Christ, he is a new creature; the old things passed away; behold new things have come."[124]

Picture this scenario. On June 7, 2006, I picked up the *Dallas Morning News*. Immediately, my mind and heart began to race. On the front cover of the business section was a picture of Ray Clark, owner of The Marketing Arm (TMA), with the title screaming in bold letters:

> The Marketing Arm muscles its way to top of industry with innovative campaigns.

What? This was the sports company I use to intern for, and had a potential promising future with, and now the company is being named the number one agency in the United States for 2006 by *Promo, the Advertising Age* magazine. My thoughts race back to the days when I worked for them. The athletes, the potential, the possibilities, the monetary fortune! Everything was coming back to my mind, wondering what could have been. In fact, my mind even began to drift when I read that TMA has "grown an amazing 729%, from $6.7 million to $56 million in net revenue last year." Well, well, well. After reading the article, my brother-in-law Garth jokingly commented, "Nice career choice." *Yeah, yeah, here I am in Dallas, as a maintenance man, working in an old apartment complex and just down the road is a sports-marketing company who, according to Ray Clark, has "gone from six clients to* 113 *and from* 60 *employees to nearly* 800 *in* 30 *cities."*[125] *The Dallas Morning News* article continued rubbing my career choice in my face, as they described the good old days when TMA used to represent professional athletes such as Scottie Pippen (NBA), Mike Modano (NHL), and Jason Sehorn (NFL). *Hey, those were the times I worked there!* Now, TMA works on deals with NASCAR, the Pizza Hut Super Bowl commercial (Miss Piggy, Jessica Simpson, and Queen Latifah), Wal-Mart and *Star Wars*, AT&T, Madonna, BMW & The Italian Job, Pepsi & *The Apprentice*. Yes, the company has grown significantly.

Was I envious? No doubt. I did the "what-if" scenario in my head. *What if I stayed with the company? What if I didn't give it up and walk away? Would I be wealthy?* A lot of questions popped into my head. I had to remind myself of the past. The fame and fortune secretly pushed me to the point where *pride* spilled out of my mouth every time I talked, and guided my steps every time I walked. I couldn't go back to that environment. It wasn't anything the company had done or any employee. Rather, it was a personal issue I knew I would struggle with for a lifetime. Pride would continually get in the way of my relationship with the Lord, so I needed to rid myself of the "old" lifestyle. No longer can I place myself in a position to give into pride.

I will always struggle with pride, but holiness is now my path of choice, a decision I have never regretted. Once I began the pursuit of holiness, there was no turning back. Even though I don't know what lies ahead of me, I walk this path according to the purpose of God. I recognize, just like each one of you, I have been called to holiness for the sake of Christ. As Paul wrote to Timothy:

> Therefore do not be ashamed of the testimony of our Lord or of me His prisoner, but join me in suffering for the gospel according to the power of God, who has saved us and called us with a holy calling, not according to our works, but according to His own purpose and grace which was granted us in Christ Jesus from all eternity.[126]

Who knows how the Lord will reveal Himself as we walk after our Holy God. But this is what makes the "pilgrim's progress" an exciting and exhilarating journey. As C.S. Lewis confirmed, "How little people know who think that holiness is dull. When one meets the real thing it is irresistible."[127]

Let us pursue this path of irresistible holiness together. All races, all denominations, all walks of life ... as long as we each place our trust in the name of Jesus Christ as the Son of God, a life of holiness is possible. And the time is *now* for the body of Christ in America to pursue a life of holiness. Out with the old and in with the new. Let us *be renewed in the spirit of our minds, and put on the new self,* "which in the likeness of God has been created in righteousness and holiness of the truth."[128]

INFLUENCE

The magnitude of God's grace allows us to look to the eternal Christ, and turn from our old way of life. We have been chosen by God to emulate His holiness. Since we have "put on the new self," we must reveal the profound characteristics of holiness to others. "Put on a heart of compassion," wear kindness, be clothed in humility, be dressed in gentleness, and put on patience.[129] We have a choice, and we choose holiness. That is how we make a difference and impact others. Even if an individual complains against us, we must forgive that person, just as Christ has forgiven us. We must know that, above all else, holiness becomes evident when we clothe ourselves in love because love unites the body of Christ.[130]

Author Eugene Peterson summarizes this approach in Colossians 3–12–14:

> So chosen by God for this new life of love, dress in the wardrobe God picked out for you: compassion, kindness, humility, quiet strength, discipline. Be even-tempered, content with second place, quick to forgive an offense. Forgive as quickly and completely as the Master forgave you. And regardless of what else you put on, wear love. It's your basic, all purpose garment. Never be without it.[131]

For me, this is where holiness is revealed—in everyday situations, in everyday conversations. It is not limited to Sunday morning services. John Walvoord, the late president of Dallas Theological Seminary, beautifully described this everyday holiness when he wrote, "The spiritual life must be lived moment by moment in relationship to the Holy Spirit as the Christian's source of strength and direction for life."[132] When the Holy Spirit is working in our lives, we are able to pursue holiness through the daily disciplines of life. The Spirit inspires and leads, as the apostle Paul wrote, when the word of Christ richly dwells in our lives.[133] So when does the Holy Spirit enter our lives in order to lead us into holiness?

In order to answer this question, let me clarify some tough issues. First of all, we need to understand the difference between the baptism of the Holy Spirit and the indwelling of the Holy Spirit. Both occur at the initial act of sanctification, however, baptism of the Holy Spirit is an immediate, one-time union with Christ. The indwelling of the Holy Spirit provides a guideline for God's work in our daily lives. Both are important to understand holiness.

Along with the baptism and indwelling of the Holy Spirit, it is also important to understand the filling of the Holy Spirit. When the believer recognizes that the Holy Spirit is free to work in his or her spiritual life, the filling of the Holy Spirit is able to "fan the flame within." The late John Walvoord contends that "the filling of the Holy Spirit is a work of God that occurs repeatedly in the life of believers, and as such it is obviously the source of sanctification as well as all spiritual fruitfulness."[134] Through the filling of the Holy Spirit, Christ's design for the everyday living of a holy life begins to take form. This is the daily process of holiness.

The theologian Robert McQuilkin also referred to this

daily process of holiness as "experiential sanctification, the outworking of one's official position in daily life."[135] This is based on the apostle Paul's call to believers to act upon their faith. "So then, my beloved ... work out your salvation with fear and trembling; for it is God who is at work in you, both to will and to work for His good pleasure."[136] It is 100% God and 100% man.[137] John Walvoord further wrote, "Though sanctification is the work of God in the heart of an individual, it is accomplished only in harmony with the human response."[138] The bottom line: holiness is possible because of Jesus, but it relies heavily on the daily disciplines of the Holy Spirit working in us. I agree with J.I. Packer:

> The Spirit works through the objective means of grace, namely, biblical truth, prayer, fellowship, worship, and the Lord's Supper, and with them through the subjective means of grace whereby we open ourselves to change, namely, thinking, listening, questioning oneself, examining oneself, admonishing oneself, sharing what is in the one's heart with others, and weighing any response they make.[139]

If we commit to knowing God with our whole being, our daily disciplines become a means of holiness. They enable us to "pursue peace with all men, and the sanctification without which no one will see the Lord."[140] We must not, however, be naïve in our thinking about holiness. Just because we pursue this life-transforming holiness, doesn't mean that everything will fall into place. On the contrary, J.I. Packer added, 'What we must realize, rather, is that any real holiness in us will be under hostile fire all the time, just as the Lord's was."[141]

The ultimate goal of holiness is to bring glory to God and "love the Lord your God, with all your heart, and with all your soul, and with all your mind, and with all your strength."[142] The theologian Melvin E. Dieter defined holiness as the "Theology of Love." He referred to the *great commandment*, to love God with all of our heart, mind, soul, and strength. It is important to understand that the Theology of Love leads to joy and peace, patience and kindness, goodness and faithfulness, gentleness, and self-control.[143] This fruit of the Spirit will be the result of the filling of the Holy Spirit

Living a life of holiness is a process, and begins with our trust in Jesus Christ. As we become aware of our inadequacies and receive the gift of grace we will desire to grow for our Lord. We will begin to reflect His holiness to others through word and deed, and they will understand and know the gospel of Jesus Christ. Allow me to explain how this continually happens in my life.

When I first arrived here at Swissaire, I had to find a balance between working and seminary. It was a constant, non-stop schedule. I was performing apartment make-readies, fulfilling maintenance requests, answering the phone, attending classes, reading the seemingly endless amounts of books required, and writing research papers. The cycle was never-ending. And don't forget I was attempting to spend quality time with my wife, family, church and friends. You know, the typical drive-thru McAmerican busy lifestyle.

I wanted to apply what I was learning in seminary and integrate it into my everyday life. That is why I went to seminary—to obtain personal insight for practical theology (study of God). I didn't necessarily want to become an expert on the Bible, but I wanted to understand the overall picture of the Scriptures. How does it all tie together? How can the Bible be applied to my own life? When I first arrived, I had a simple knowledge of the Scriptures. But there was a depth I was missing. I felt I was growing at a slow pace in my walk with the Lord, and I needed a jump start to further my Christian growth. The answer was not seminary. It was being intentional about studying the sixty-six books of the Bible.

In the spring of 2002, I took a class that had a significant impact on my views of the Scriptures. The professor asked the class if we could define the gospel. He continued by pointing out that, if the gospel was to be a message concerning the Person of Jesus Christ, then we should be able to articulate, to others, who Jesus was based on the Scriptures. I knew what I believed about Jesus and how His death and resurrection granted me eternal life, but, sadly enough, I didn't know if I could recall passages in order to effectively communicate this to others. As the professor continued his lesson, I was challenged to grow in this area of my walk with the Lord. It was time to obey Christ's words in the Great Commission, when He said, "Go therefore and make disciples of all the nations, baptizing them in the name of the Father and the Son and the Holy Spirit, teaching them to observe all that I commanded you; and lo; I am with you always, even to the end of the age."[144]

So, over the course of time at seminary, I began to understand how to make a difference for the kingdom of God by sharing the most important thing in my life with others—my relationship with Christ. No more days without being intentional about my relationship with Christ. It was time to share the gospel with others. Some of my biggest frustrations while in school were the personal struggles of overcoming the student mentality. I have no doubt that God called me to study His word in an academic environment; however, life did exist outside the institutional walls. There is more to life than books and dissertations and much more than these things to Christianity.

A good example of how to apply study to practical life is shown by the apostle Paul. For two years at the school of Tyrannus in Ephesus, he taught and trained twelve disciples to better understand the "Way of Christ." It is important to note that these individuals were *studying and presenting the Way* (the gospel) to those around them. They didn't allow the knowledge to swell up their heads; rather they were deflating it with practical efforts. How do we know Paul and the students impacted others during their school time? Because in Acts, Paul wrote, "He (Paul) did this for two years, giving everyone in the province of Asia, Jews as well as Greeks, ample opportunity to hear the Message of the Master."[145] *(parentheses refer to author input)*

This was only possible if they believed and understood the gospel message in their own lives. Did you catch that? This is important not to overlook. How do we expect other lives' to change if we don't comprehend it ourselves? If the message is a mist in our own mind, imagine the foggy cloud it will be for others?[146] Well, I decided to stretch myself. So, over the course of two and a half years (my time to finish my master's program), I furthered my understanding of who Jesus was in my life and how He has made a difference for me.

Some of you might be thinking, "Not me, man. I don't have the gift of evangelism! Don't talk to me about sharing Christ with others. I will leave that to the over-excited and extreme Christian." Let me ask each of you, when we are faced with an opportunity to share about Jesus, do we desire to express our testimony of what He has done in our lives? We are to be responsible witnesses for the sake of Christ. Christ addressed these very issues of evangelism and missions to His disciples about the Great Commission when

He said, "But you will receive power when the Holy Spirit has come upon you; and you shall be My witnesses both in Jerusalem, and in all Judea and Samaria, and even to the remotest part of the earth."[147] Just like the disciples in the first century, we too have been given the power of the Holy Spirit to make a difference to those around us.

To push myself outside of my comfort zone, I copied the Acts 1:8 passage on a post-note in my maintenance shop. I wanted to be a witness for Jesus. It wasn't easy to share the gospel, nor did it come naturally. In fact, whenever I knew I was going to say "Jesus Christ," I found it quite difficult. Why is it so hard to say Jesus aloud to someone? But, the more that I invested time in the Word of God, the more I understood my role in the body of Christ. For example, as I was working in apartment #127, I described who Jesus was to a Spanish-speaking drywall contractor by spray painting a gospel message on the walls. Another time, I presented a bilingual Bible to a plumbing contractor, and walked him through the Scripture passages concerning the message of Jesus Christ. (And I don't speak Spanish!) It was never easy, and I was nervous every time.

This is exactly why Paul asked others to pray that the gospel message be made clear to whom he talks with.[148] He didn't want the message of Jesus to be conveyed in a confusing, difficult, or overwhelming manner. Rather, Paul wanted Jesus to be understood. This is exactly why, when each opportunity arises, we need to be ready and prepared to express a simple message/testimony for all to hear. Paul encouraged each of us to have this intentionally equipped mindset, when he wrote, "Conduct yourselves with wisdom toward outsiders, making the most of the opportunity."[149] We can't let the opportunities slip by. But we can only be effective when we have engrossed ourselves into the

Scriptures. So, do we really know what the Bible says about Jesus? When we do, as followers of Jesus, we can graciously respond to others. The apostle Paul wrote, "Let your speech always be with grace, as though seasoned with salt, so that you will know how you should respond to each person."[150]

Please remember one thing, if any individual we talk to is to place their trust in Christ, it is because the Spirit prepared the individual and softened their heart. It is not because of our smooth talking or being politically correct. The Holy Spirit is the One who will "close the deal." Over the course of my time in Dallas, I wanted to see the Holy Spirit move in mighty ways. I wanted others to not only hear the love of Jesus, but to see it firsthand.

Where I live in downtown Dallas, our apartments are surrounded with the poor and impoverished, a.k.a. the homeless. Constantly I am burdened for these individuals and their walk with the Lord, but how can I impact these individuals for the sake of Christ? Immediately, some of you might think I went to the extreme and stood on a street corner holding a sign announcing judgment and condemnation for all those who don't believe in Jesus. But I didn't do that. Rather, I wanted to be intentional and share the love of Jesus through my *actions*. I wanted *holiness to reveal itself as the daily outcome of my faith in Jesus Christ, during which I unconditionally love and serve Him with all of my heart, soul, and mind.*

In 104 degree weather, I hopped on an old friend's three-wheeled bicycle and went to the neighborhood grocery store. I loaded down the wire-basket attached to the tricycle with bottles of water. And, for the remainder of the afternoon, I peddled around a five to six block area looking for those in need of one essential thing—water. At first, many were hesitant, but almost everyone took the water. It was too hot not to. While lying down on the sidewalk, Billy Joe just looked up at me in shock. In all reality, she didn't care why I was doing what I was doing. Billy Joe was just thirsty, and at that point in time, the good Lord had provided a blue Aquafina to quench her thirst.

I continued my "water-distribution" journey on and around Swiss Avenue. Across at the run-down laundromat, I met a man name Cole who knew the former owner of the tricycle I was riding. Further down the street, children playing in their cement front-yard came running up to me asking for water. (At that moment, I felt like the ice cream man minus the bells and whistles.) At one point in my ride, I passed a man sanding kitchen cabinets in his garage. It had to have been at least 110 degrees in the garage. I asked him, "What in the world are you doing in this heat?" He responded, "What in the world are you doing with all that water? I tossed my neighbor a water bottle and said, "Just handing out free water." He smiled and showed his gratitude with a simple wave. Time and time again, people all over the neighborhood were astonished that I was distributing water for free. Even the guys at the halfway house, Leonard and "Forrest Gump" enjoyed the refreshing water. Anything to quench their thirst on a hot summer day.

One guy in particular stands out in my mind. His name was Jerome. Here was a seasoned homeless man sitting outside of the closed-down Dollar Store. I handed him the water. He accepted, and immediately began to pour out his life story to me. I didn't necessarily ask, but he offered. He could quote more Scripture than I could ever imagine. He was the son of a preacher, a father of many children, a man recently let out of prison, a jack-of-all-trades. Jerome was a character who was always looking to talk and, boy, could he talk. I just listened, occasionally offering some feedback.

As we parted ways, he thanked me for the water, and

made one last comment. He thanked me for sharing the gospel of Jesus Christ. I told him I never expressed who Jesus Christ was nor did I explain what He has done in my life. I said I was simply handing out water. He disagreed. He said I was doing what the body of Christ was instructed to do, and that was to reflect the Head of the body of Christ—Jesus. Jerome was right. At that moment, I began to understand the words of Jesus to His disciples when He said:

> I was hungry and you fed me,
> I was thirsty and you gave me a drink,
> I was homeless and you gave me a room,
> I was shivering and you gave me clothes,
> I was sick and you stopped to visit,
> I was in prison and you came to me.[151]

Here, a man on the streets of Dallas was encouraged by my actions. He said he saw Jesus in my life—humbling words to hear. Even though I hadn't preached Jesus, I made a difference in this man's life for a brief twenty-five minutes, and showed him the love of Christ through my daily actions. According to the man on the street, the holiness of God was being reflected to those around him.

Because I was willing to go through the process of being available, the Lord used me for His glory. While in Dallas, there has been a sense of growth and development in my life. Remember the parking lot process? It has taken time. It has been a progression. But my love for Jesus has grown. How did this come about? With The Marketing Arm's downtown office building looming in the distance, I took the time to learn the Word of God. I took the time to pray. I took the time to fast. I pursued Him, and listened to the

Holy Spirit's leading. Whether I had a conversation with a professional plumber or handed out water to the homeless, God revealed to me that I can share Christ with others. By His grace, I am able to have an impact for His kingdom in the midst of inner-city Dallas.

In this journey of holiness, Paul encouraged each of us to keep our eyes on Christ. He wrote, "Whatever you do in word or deed, do all in the name of the Lord Jesus, giving thanks through Him to God the Father."[152] Gratitude will continue to keep our perspective on the bigger, eternal picture. Because when we pursue personal holiness, we will long for something more, something called glorification or "ultimate sanctification." Glorification is the complete and perfect state of holiness that "occurs when the believer is totally transformed into the likeness of Jesus."[153] We won't reach that state of holiness until we meet Christ face-to-face in eternity, but the apostle John confirmed, "Beloved, now we are children of God, and it has not appeared as yet what we will be. We know that when He appears, we will be like Him, because we will see Him just as He is."[154] In this permanent holiness stage, we will see Christ in His completeness and experience the glory of God. One theologian wrote, "All the amazing blessings of our salvation, including our sanctification, have as their final goal the praise of the glory of God. Nothing in all of history will reveal the fullness of God's perfections as brilliantly as will the completed glorification of His people." [155]

A SERVANT'S REQUEST

Results from divine response

47. The response towards Your people O, God
Will glow forever through an unconditional,
Never ending burning bush of love.

48. And may Your never ending devotion ignite a flame within Your people,
By the power of the Spirit:
Let us return to the work of faith,
Let us persevere each day with hope,
And let us maintain a labor of love.

49. Where restoration awaits Your people O God,
Guaranteed upon commitment.

50. May all Your people sing praises of thanksgiving,
To the Eternal and Absolute One.

51. Whose everlasting nature of restoration beats a rhythm aloud,
In order for Your people to dance in praise.

52. Praise the name of God!
From the test of time, Your name will stand alone,
And the great and mighty God;
Will be exalted by Your people on high;
A name worthy to be praised.
Praise the name of God!

DIVINE RESPONSE
In Pursuit of *Results*

My place of refuge is located within the heart of the Swissaire Apartments' parking lot—the maintenance shop. It was built in the 1950s along with the rest of the apartment building. While it is neat and tidy, it is not a twenty-first century shop. Surrounded by the tenants' vehicles, and adjacent to the laundry room, my shop has a lot of character and memories. On a shelf in the shop's front room, there is a historic display of pieces and parts organized to show how they once served this building. When I first came here, this shop was anything but organized. While putting the shop together, I found piles of old hardware, tools and fixtures that were discarded for newer parts and thrown in a heap and forgotten about. Silly as it seems, I thought they deserved better than a scrap pile. These small pieces of history had served the building well, and I decided to keep some of them. So on my shelf, I have: a broken shut-off valve, an old brass door knob that looks original to the building, and a cracked and weathered parking lot sign, to name a few.

Next to my historical display, to the right of these items

beyond repair are more memories, collected over the past eight years—license plates. Not antique or collectible, the plates represent each state where my wife and I have lived or visited. The *Lone Star State*, the *Volunteer State*, the *Crossroads of America*, the *Land of* 10,000 *Lakes,* and the *Peaceful Garden State* are all represented. These well-traveled plates act as a reminder of the Lord working in my life. They are miniature billboards representing life-long lessons. Each plate conjures up a different emotion, a different memory. Most importantly, they reflect my journey with the Lord where results are witnessed in and throughout many stages of life.

We mustn't forget how the Lord has worked in our lives. Take, for example, in the Old Testament, when Joshua instructed his fellow countrymen to gather twelve stones and pile them in the middle of the Jordan River. Why? "Because the waters of the Jordan were cut off before the ark of the covenant of the Lord; when it crossed the Jordan, the waters of the Jordan were cut off."[156] The "memorial markers"[157] were to act as a reminder of God's faithfulness while the Israelites safely crossed over a "dry" Jordan River. The same goes for my license plates. Each one served as a memorable testimony to the Lord.

My childhood and college years were spent in Indiana. I traveled to and from North Dakota to visit the relatives in a quaint farming community. My wife grew up in Minnesota. As newlyweds we went to Tennessee where we lived for a year. We now find ourselves in Texas, as a small family with two joyful and energized young daughters.

Over the course of our lives, we each have all felt "1DRFL" or "GR8,," and other days we have had "ENUF" and ran on "MT2DAY." We have ridden over the bumps in life's road, with a lot of potholes and detours. But we shouldn't let the everyday highway detour our walk with the

Lord. We are to press on and grow in our knowledge and understanding of Jesus. The author of Hebrews wrote:

> So come on, let's leave the preschool finger-painting exercises on Christ and get on with the grand work of art. Grow up in Christ. The basic foundational truths are in place: turning your back on "salvation by self-help" and turning in trust toward God; baptismal instructions; laying on of hands; resurrection of the dead; eternal judgment. God helping us, we'll stay true to all that. But there's so much more. Let's get on with it![158]

The time is now to move forward in our relationship with God. Not backwards. And this is exactly why we mustn't forget the times in the past when the Lord has worked, especially when each of us is faced with present struggles and hardships. That is why Joshua requested that the Israelites build a memorial of stones. That is why I have displayed the license plates in my maintenance shop. The stones and license plates are to act as reminders of God's faithfulness in our lives. Why do we need reminders? We need them because we, as humans, tend to forget the results of the Lord working in our lives. The author of Hebrews warned:

> Once people have seen the light, gotten a taste of heaven and been part of the work of the Holy Spirit, once they've personally experienced the sheer goodness of God's Word and the powers breaking in on us—if they turn their backs on it, washing theirs hands of the whole thing, well, they can't start over as if nothing happened. That's impossible. Why, they've re-crucified

> Jesus! They've repudiated him in public. Parched ground that soaks up the rain and then produces an abundance of carrots and corn for its gardener gets God's "Well done!" But if it produces weeds and thistles, it's more likely to get cussed out. Fields like that are burned, not harvested."[159]

Have we turned our back on the Lord? Have we fallen to the wayside? The author of Hebrews decided to address these questions with a positive approach and answer. Even though he knew life as followers of Christ would be difficult, the caring pastor wrote words of encouragement to the church at Thessalonica.[160] The author still believed in the Thessalonians. He said, "But, beloved, we are convinced of better things concerning you, and things that accompany salvation, though we are speaking in this way."[161] Or in other words, "But I am sure you people would never do that!"[162]

Can this be true? Can we *practically* prevent our walk with the Lord from going back to the early stages of a Christian? Also, can we avoid a time period of stagnate growth?

> How can we see the results of our spiritual growth in the Lord?
> Is it possible?

Without a doubt, to all of these questions—*yes, yes, yes, yes, and yes!* Whether we see God's rewards here on earth, or after we've entered Heaven, God *will* reward our daily obedience to Him. The key to knowing and experiencing a *divine response* from God is pursuing a new and living way through *faith, hope and love*.

This is exactly why I pray that the Holy Spirit sweeps

across America and inspires mankind to uphold a passionate perspective of *faith*,[163] to maintain a life of promising *hope*,[164] and to journey through everyday routine with *love*.[165] These practical steps toward restoration will assist members of the body of Christ in drawing near to the Lord[166] and develop a more personal and intimate fellowship with Him.[167] The results are inevitable and will be fantastic.

I challenge each of you, skeptical or not, to test everything against Scripture and be open to the Holy Spirit's move within our nation. Break the mold of your lukewarm life. Be willing to be restored in the presence of the Lord. Know that by the blood of our Lord and Savior Jesus Christ we, as the body of Christ, have permission to enter the holy presence of our almighty God.[168] Christ is the means to approaching God. As followers of Jesus Christ, in order to comprehend the calling for us to live our lives in a new and distinct way, we must understand the importance of coming before the Lord with faith, hope and love in this spiritual journey. We will then experience firsthand the results of a just God working in our lives.

FAITH

As a simple reminder that my life is a "WRK UV FTH," all I need to do is take a quick glance at the Tennessee license plate in my shop. This title plate of the Volunteer State immediately triggers memories of my personal experiences and how the Lord revealed Himself in my life. My wife and I moved to Tennessee without jobs, with no place to live and no clear vision of our future. We were heading to Tennessee by faith.

Faith is the fuel that allows us to see, firsthand, the Lord working in our lives. It is the ignition that turns on the engine for everyday life. Faith trusts in the work of God, and trusts He is working in our lives through Christ. Faith is defined as believing the unseen. It is this firm faith that allows us to be confident in what we place our hope in. With faith, we are granted confidence in the eternal things. Faith also allows us to fight the battles of everyday life. Faith allows us to take risks and "get out of the boat." Picture a person of faith in your mind's eye. Their lives don't correlate with the expected and prepared, but they do fall into place according to the will of God. When we are willing to "draw near with a sincere heart in full assurance of faith,"[169] "faith is the firm foundation under everything that makes life worth living."[170]

By nature, I am an optimist. I am a glass-is-half-full kind of guy, but I carry optimism with determination. If I wasn't sure how to get to Nashville, I had to be willing to get directions. I was not going to sit and wait for the Lord to drop a map in my lap. Not because I'm impatient or because I lacked faith in God, but because I had a responsibility to be faithful with what I knew to be true in my life. According to the author of Hebrews, we will see and experience "better things" from the Lord, when we avoid a "sluggish" lifestyle.[171] We mustn't be lazy.

In deciding whether or not to go to Tennessee, the Spirit served as my guide. I had to obey. It was time. My faith maintained a simple, yet practical outlook of 100% man and 100% God. [172] This can only mean—we are to do something with what we believe in. It was time to put my faith to work.[173] In the New Testament, James wrote:

> Dear friends, do you think you'll get anywhere in this if you learn all the right words but never do anything? Does merely talking about faith indicate that a person really has it? For instance,

> you come upon an old friend dressed in rags and half-starved and say, "Good morning, friend! Be clothed in Christ! Be filled with the Holy Spirit!" and walk off without providing so much as a coat or a cup of soup—where does that get you? Isn't it obvious that God-talk without God-acts is outrageous nonsense?
>
> I can already hear one of you agreeing by saying, "Sounds good. You take care of the faith department, I'll handle the works department."
>
> Not so fast. You can no more show me your works apart from your faith than I can show you my faith apart from my works. Faith and works, works and faith, fit together hand in glove.[174]

Faith calls us into action. A faithful action that leads each one of us into the inheritance of God's promise.[175]

Action is not the means to God, but displays the faith which we have in God.

How will the world know that we are believers in Christ if we do nothing to proclaim our faith? In her book *The Adventure of Faith*, Mabel N. Thurston described faith-in-action. She broke it down into five simple steps:

> The need.
>
> My own limited resources and wisdom. I may be able to do a little, but that little is nothing at all compared to what the situation requires.

> God's will—which is that every one of His children should have what is necessary for life.
>
> God's infinite resources and wisdom.
>
> His eagerness to help at the point where my ability ends.[176]

God will reveal Himself and His will for each of our lives if we allow Him to.

In America, our faith typically fluctuates based on "signs" that we get from the Lord, signs that prove His response to our needs and wants. Yet, unlike the Pharisees of the first century who tested Him, our faithfulness should not be dependant on signs. "Sighing deeply in His spirit, (Jesus) said, 'Why does this generation seek for a sign? Truly I say to you, no sign will be given to this generation.'"[177] *(parentheses refer to author input)* Yes, it would be wonderful to see our future revealed on the front page of the newspaper. For some reason, I think this would lead to problems. Look at the people who have been handed millions of dollars from winning the lottery. Their guaranteed financial future has been handed to them on a platter. Yet, when a "sign" is handed to us, things tend to fall apart. That is why we must place our faith in Christ alone, and walk accordingly.

Signs of success are not necessarily indications of our faithfulness in the Lord. Picture a small church in North Dakota, twenty parishioners strong, greatly serving the Lord. Simply because they are small in number, doesn't mean that their impact for the Lord is insignificant. Just because an elderly believer develops cancer doesn't indicate that he was unfaithful to the Lord. Signs of a blessed life are by no means an indication of favoritism by God. Just look at the life of Job. Job was a man "blameless, upright, fearing God and turning from evil,"[178] and yet he was allowed by God to be tested by Satan.[179] As a beautiful example for all to live by, even amidst the killing of sheep, servants, camels, sons, and daughters, Job continued to bless the name of the Lord. He remained faithful to the Lord when he said:

> Naked I came from my mother's womb, and
> naked I shall return there.
> The Lord gave and the Lord has taken away.
> Blessed be the name of the Lord.[180]

What about the times in Scripture when people of faith requested signs from the Lord? In these specific situations, signs were justified because of their motives. For example, in the Book of Judges, Gideon received a Divine commission to "deliver Israel from the hand of Midian,"[181] As he was working in the wine press, the Lord told him that things were going to change. It was time for Gideon to leave his normal routine and lead Israel to deliverance. But Gideon needed reassurance that the Lord was behind him 100%. Who wouldn't? When a person is called to defeat an army 120,000 strong with only 300 chosen men? Gideon requested two signs: a wet fleece and a dry fleece. It was recorded:

> Gideon said to God, "If this is right, if you are using me to save Israel as you've said, then look: I'm placing a fleece of wool on the threshing floor. If dew is on the fleece only, but the floor is dry, then I know that you will use me to save Israel, as you said."

> That's what happened. When he got up early the next morning, he wrung out the fleece—enough dew to fill a bowl with water!
>
> Then Gideon said to God, "Don't be impatient with me, but let me say one more thing. I want to try another time with the fleece. But this time let the fleece stay dry, while the dew drenches the ground."
>
> God made it happen that very night. Only the fleece was dry while the ground was wet with dew.[182]

Signs can come in big and small ways. As much as I wanted to believe the Lord wanted us in Tennessee, I still struggled with the decision. So I prayed for confirmation that this was what the Lord wanted. I was driving on Highway 69, outside of the small town of Alexandria, Indiana, and approached an old white Cadillac. As I gazed at the familiar crest adorning the trunk, I noticed the license plate. It was a Tennessee license plate. I looked at it for what seemed like a minute. "GO 2 TN." I'm sorry, what? "GO 2 TN." I took a double take as the Caddie pulled off on an exit ramp. Did God just answer my prayers with a license plate? Yes, He might have. I then felt confident enough about two things: 1) I can tell Laura we are moving to Nashville and 2) God, apparently, drives an old white Cadillac!

Did I simply believe in the license plate or did I have faith to do something about my confirmation? What's the difference between these questions? Throughout the Scriptures, the Greek words of "belief" and "faith" are almost always used interchangeable. A good example can be found when we search for the word "believe." Three essential verses come to my mind where "faith" and "believe" can be interchanged:

John 3:16	"For God so loved the world, that He gave His only begotten Son, that whoever *has faith* in Him shall not perish, but have eternal life."
John 5:24	"Truly, truly, I say to you, he who hears My word, and whoever *has faith* in Him who sent Me, has eternal life, and does not come into judgment , but has passed out of death into life."
Acts 16:31	"They said, whoever '*has faith*' in the Lord Jesus, and you will be saved, you and your household."

We can do the same for the word "believe." If we were to find three "faith" verses, we can interchange them with the word "believe."

Romans 4:5	"But to the one who does not, but believes in Him who justifies the ungodly, his believing is accounted for righteousness."
Ephesians 2:8–9	"For by grace you have been saved through believing, and that not of yourselves, it is the gift of God, not of works, lest anyone should boast."
Hebrews 11:1	"Now believing is the assurance of things hoped for, the conviction of things not seen."

Is there even a difference between the word "belief" and the word "faith?" In the American English language there is a distinct difference and this is an essential key. Allow me to explain. A person can believe in God. A person can even believe in Jesus Christ. Often, though, this belief is only on an intellectual level... it lacks the spiritual depth that faith provides. Mabel Thurston wrote:

> Belief is intellectual and need not, necessarily, commit one to action. You may believe that travel by air is safe, but you are not, by that belief, committed to the use of airplanes whenever you travel. I may "believe" in God—believe, that is, that there is a God—and that belief never change my life in any degree. But I cannot have faith in God without doing something about it! Genuine faith always involves self-committal to the God in Whom I have faith, and the God to Whom I commit myself tests that faith every day of my life.[18]

Faith in the church in America must be more than believing in something. Believing in something is easy. It doesn't require us to do anything. But faith in God calls us to something more. It calls us to get dirty and uncomfortable. Faith calls us to act upon the direction given to us by the Lord. Just as Paul encouraged the church at Thessalonica, we are also to continue with our "work of faith."[184] At times this "work of faith" is difficult and cannot be explained. But faith must be pursued, regardless of how the world perceives our actions. When faith is pursued, we begin to know and experience the Lord as our Savior.

No one was going to make me to go to Tennessee. In

fact, I wouldn't receive any accolades or awards for leaving. I took action and God revealed Himself through my steps of faith. Our lives are not meant to be spent dwelling on the missteps and failures of the past. While we can look back occasionally at lessons learned and identify the various spiritual stepping stones in our lives, we must acknowledge that life was designed for the present. Because there is so much to know about and experience with the Lord each and every day, I didn't want to miss any opportunity to draw closer to Him. Therefore, with an awareness and understanding of the *conditions of faith*,[185] I fully invested in this journey. As a result, my life would be transformed into a truly dedicated follower of Jesus Christ.

Friends, please don't think it was easy. I was fully aware of the *obstacles to faith* that I would face. Roadblocks came, and it was up to me to decide whether or not I would rely on Him to see me through. If I decided to turn to Him, the *trials of faith* would be overcome and thrown to the wayside. If I turned to myself, the journey of faith would get that much more difficult.

No one could explain what I would experience on a personal level. No one could predict it. No sermon could outline it. Only the process of living out my faith would allow me to understand. I was able to grow in my own faith, and slowly, I understood the *process of faith*.

Living by faith is exciting and thrilling. It is a never-ending journey during which the Lord slowly unveils more of Himself. At any given moment, it is up to us to act upon our beliefs. With the future unknown, strive to make the most of each day, and see the *results of the Lord working through faith* in your own life. Therefore, when we work out our faith, we will always be able to walk in our own "maintenance shops" and glance at the memorable license plates of our lives.

HOPE

The phrase "HLDFST 2 HOPE" is what comes to mind every time I see the Indiana license plate in the shop. In 1989, in the small town of Middlebury, Indiana, my parents started a family-owned Ace Hardware store from scratch. My dad, Larry, was anxiously excited for what lay ahead. My mom, Gloria, was hopeful for what was to come. My brother, Shannon, was energized by the possibilities. My sister, Janaé, was eager to explore the unknown and, as a ten-year-old boy, I was thrilled to experience the aisles of a new store. We were all very hopeful for the future of our store.

For many Americans, hope is in what lies just around the corner. Tomorrow could be my lucky day! Next year could be the big year. To many in the world, the United States is the personification of hope. It is the land of opportunity. A land where we can do anything we put our mind to. This is the land where a man can live the "American dream." But, my friends, if we place our hope in the temporary things, we will only be disappointed. Nothing will ever be enough.

Over the course of eighteen years, our family has waited for the business to unfold in consistency and profit. Since the store's first day, Martin Ace Home Center has always been in the business of survival. In fact, the pursuit of more retail business has never stopped. There has been no choice. Cash flow is always a necessity of survival. With the store having started from the ground floor, my parents are constantly paying out for more product, shelving, vans, forklifts, trucks, rent, employees—all necessary payments. Unfortunately, business has never been a guarantee, and the customers' commitment comes and goes.

So where do we put our hope? One thing is for sure, growing up in Indiana was a time for my family and I to live in expectation (hope). We trusted that our hope for more business would be fulfilled. It was unclear of when it would happen, but over time, I realized my hope was placed in the everyday business. However, the hope I was waiting for cannot be provided by human effort. Hope doesn't lie within the amount of customers that walk through the front door. Nor can hope come from the cash that is placed in the registers. Therefore, hope must be found in the one and only blessed hope, Jesus Christ. He is the anchor of our soul and allows us to remain sure and steadfast in a world of fabricated satisfactions.

The Indiana license plate in the shop, "HLDFST 2 HOPE," reminds me of two essential elements—patience and perseverance. According to the author of Hebrews, we are to be "imitators of those who through ... patience inherit the promises."[186] The promises of hope are designed for us to "expect something beneficial in the future."[187] This something beneficial is that our "citizenship is in heaven from which also we eagerly wait for a Savior, the Lord Jesus Christ."[188] Do we believe that the eternal promise for our lives will be fulfilled? One way to find out is through the words of Scripture. The apostle Paul wrote, "Whatever was written in earlier times was written for our instruction, so that through perseverance and the encouragement of the Scriptures we might have hope."[189] Take the life of Abraham for example. The Lord promised His servant, "I will surely bless you and I will surely multiply you." Did Abraham ever see the results of God's promise? The author of Hebrews wrote, "And so, having patiently waited, he (Abraham) obtained the promise." God doesn't lie.[190] He will fulfill His promise for those who believe in Him. Let us be encouraged to "take hold of the hope set before us."[191] For when we come before the Lord with patient hope, the Lord finds favor with us.[192]

Hope also requires perseverance. To persevere is hard, especially when life throws us curves. Just ask my dad, mom and brother as they work day in and day out to survive in the world of retail. In 1997, Ace Hardware Corporation came to my family and suggested we close the doors for good. We had been in business for eight years, and according to the corporate representatives, the numbers didn't add up. They didn't think we could make it financially. Looking around at all of our family members, I remember being confused. Is this what God had in store for our family? Were we really going to go out of business?

One look at my dad that night and I knew he had already made up his mind. Our family declined their "expert" advice, dug our heels into the local community, and pressed on. My dad went out shopping for business. A new housing contractor entered the picture and the store was saved. But we couldn't rely solely on one lumber contractor to get us through the tough times. Our family began to diversify. We identified more of the needs within our Amish-community, and we pursued them with every ounce of Martin energy we had. Martin Ace Home Center truly had become the "Crossroads" of our town. Not only had we become a hardware store, but we also were a lumberyard, a floral and gift store and, eventually, we developed a truck delivery system for the Amish. The everyday business was, and still is, an endless and tireless journey. Some days are harder than others. But on any given day, good or bad, I truly believe my dad looks back to that day in '97, when all the lights in the store, save one, were out and my family listened as the two reps tried to convince my dad to sell everything. They wanted us to quit. My dad refused and, through faith and perseverance, he led our family through the thick and thin of the next nine years.

So what pushes a person, like my father, to persevere? The answer is quite simple—we have to know what we are striving for. Why do we press on? We need to know what the end result is. The author of Hebrews encouraged his fellow believers to be diligent in their faith in Christ "so as to realize the full assurance of hope until the end."[193] We must "hold fast our confidence and the boast of our hope firm until the end."[194] As followers of Jesus Christ, we are assured an eternal inheritance in the kingdom of God. So we must "HLDFST" to this hope until we are in heaven, eternally, with Jesus. Peter agreed when he wrote,

> Blessed be the God and Father of our Lord Jesus Christ, who according to His great mercy has caused us to be born again to a living hope through the resurrection of Jesus Christ from the dead, to obtain an inheritance which is imperishable and undefiled and will not fade away, reserved in heaven for you, who are protected by the power of God through faith for a salvation ready to be revealed in the last time.[195]

Hope allows us to overcome the daily woes of life. Worries and anxieties do nothing but bring headaches. We are to "be anxious for nothing." Even when life is constantly bringing us struggles, whether we are attempting to make ends meet at the hardware store, loving our kids as a stay-at-home mom, or trying to meet the time deadlines as a tractor-trailer driver, we must "HLDFST." Our eyes should be fixed on "whatever is true, whatever is honorable, whatever is right, whatever is pure, whatever is lovely, whatever is of good repute, if there is any excellence and if anything worthy of praise, dwell on these things." More specifically, we need to persevere with a perspective on Jesus Christ.

For myself, in order to persevere and hold fast, I need to clarify what I know to be true about Jesus. I recognize that the days are fleeting. We aren't guaranteed anything in life. Therefore, with a world that has ever-changing morals and values, I recognize I need to remain firm in what I have been given and believe in. I am tired of running from what I need to be doing. Therefore, I am ready and willing. Regardless of the means, I am willing to do whatever it takes to *revive others in their relationship with the Lord Jesus Christ.* No more looking for hope in areas that I know won't bring satisfaction. I feel called to convey this message of revival to others and, if required, I would give my life to do so. I am that passionate about revival and restoration in the United States. Dr. Martin Luther King Jr. said, "If you can't find a cause to die for, you've got nothing to live for."[196]

I know that I cannot stop with what I am doing. I cannot stray away from the path to which the Lord has called me. I love what motivates me each and every day. I am to "HLDFST" with patience and perseverance.

> I'm part of the fellowship of the unashamed
> I have stepped over the line.
> The decision has been made.
> I'm a disciple of Jesus Christ.
> I won't look back, let up, slow down, back away,
> or be still.
> My past is redeemed, my present makes sense, my
> future is secure.
> I'm finished and done with low living, sight
> walking, small planning, smooth knees,

colorless dreams, tamed visions, mundane talking,
cheap living, and dwarfed goals.
I no longer need preeminence, prosperity,
position, promotions, plaudits, or popularity.
I don't have to be right, first, tops, recognized,
praised, regarded, or rewarded.
I now live by faith, lean on His presence, walk by
patience, lift by prayer, and labor by power.
My face is set, my gait is fast, my goal is heaven,
my road narrow, my way rough, my
companions few, my Guide reliable, my mission clear.
I cannot be bought, deluded, or delayed.
I will not flinch in the face of sacrifice, hesitate in
the presence of the adversary, negotiate at the table of
the enemy, or meander in the maze of mediocrity.
I won't give up, shut up, let up, until I have stayed
up, stored up, prayed up, paid up,
preached up for the cause for the cause of Christ.
I am a disciple of Jesus.
I must go till He comes, give till I drop, preach till
all know, and work till He stops me.
And when He comes for His own, He will have no
problem recognizing me–
my banner will be clear![197]

With the help of daily Scripture readings, we all can be encouraged to have hope in Jesus. Then with hope engrained in our hearts and minds, we are able to entrust our attitudes and actions over to Jesus. Like a domino effect, the message of hope becomes contagious to others. Others will desire to know more about Jesus, the blessed assurance of hope. With understanding patience and perseverance in our lives, we can explain how we "… hold fast the confession of our hope without wavering, for He who promised is faithful."[198]

LOVE

As I glimpse at the Texas license plate in my workshop, I am reminded to "LABR 4 LUV." This is the final piece of the three-part puzzle essential to seeing, firsthand, the Lord move in our lives. It makes up the third pillar of faith, hope and love. Texas is my home for now and it's the birthplace of my two daughters Maya and Nadia. There is a lot of love in my life here, and even more so, as I deepen my relationship with the Lord.

Love is easier said than done. It is something we all long for, yet struggle to give. We are in a constant search for love. In today's society, love is thought to be found in intimate relationships; yet we become heartbroken. Love is thought to be discovered through approval from others; yet we get rejected. Love is thought to be intertwined with committed friendships; yet our friends sometimes replace us with someone else. And, just when we think we have found love, it skirts away. The problem is that we aren't really sure where to find love. The Black Eyed Peas, in one of their songs, profoundly ask "Where is the Love?"

> I feel the weight of the world on my shoulder
> As I'm getting older y'all people get colder
> Most of us only care about money makin'
> Selfishness got us following the wrong direction
> Wrong information always shown by the media
> Negative images is the main criteria
> Infecting their young minds faster than bacteria
> Kids wanna act like what they see in the cinema

Whatever happened to the values of humanity
Whatever happened to the fairness and equality
Instead of spreading love, we're spreading animosity
Lack of understanding, leading us away from unity
That's the reason why sometimes I'm feeling under
That's the reason why sometimes I'm feeling down
It's no wonder why sometimes I'm feeling under
I gotta keep my faith alive, until love is found
People killing people dying
Children hurtin' you hear them crying
Can practice what you preach
Would you turn the other cheek?
Father, father, father help us
Send some guidance from above
Cause people got me got me questioning
Where is the love?[199]

In order to find true love, we need to know where to look. Well, look no further. Stop searching and turn your eyes to God. God *is* love. How do we know God is the definition of love? We know because God demonstrated His love to us through the death, burial and resurrection of His Son, Jesus Christ. God is the source of love. In order to "keep ourselves in the love of God,"[200] we are to rely on the Holy Spirit and keep His commandments. These commandments are to *love God & love others.* As Christ loved God and others, we are also required to do the same. Love is meant to be given away with all of our heart, and with all of our soul, and with all of our mind, and with all of our strength. The bottom line is, "Our actions illustrate our love."[201] Many are hungry and thirsty, sick and naked. Can we honestly say we are doing anything about it? Are we devoted to one another in love? Are we willing to contribute to the needs of other believers? The apostle John confirmed love in action when he wrote, "Let's not just talk about love, let's practice real love. This is the only way we'll know we're living truly, living in God's reality."[202] The reality of living for the Lord is to "put on love."[203] For when we clothe ourselves in love, we have created the "perfect bond of unity"[204] amongst the body of Christ.

Charlie is my good friend at Swissaire who understands love and the importance of unity within the body of Christ. He has lived here for forty years. What inspires one man to stay in one apartment complex for four decades? He could have paid off a house by now. But the answer is quite simple—the community of love. Within this quaint "urban cottage"[205] setting Charlie knows, for the most part, what to expect from the other tenants—love. There is an actual sense and feel at Swissaire for what the author of Hebrews wrote: "Let us consider how to consider how to stimulate one another to love and good deeds, not forsaking our own assembling together, as is the habit of some, but encouraging one another; and all the more as you see the day drawing near."[206] This wouldn't happen if Charlie wasn't intentional about investing into each of our lives in a unique manner. He calls us to get out of our "shells" called apartments and live as a community.

One day, as I was doing some paperwork, Charlie entered the apartment office. He had that look on his face. He was on a mission, and it was a mission that spoke loud and clear to me, especially when I noticed the pair of toenail clippers in his hand. I knew what he wanted. With his age and bad back, Charlie struggled to bend over and touch his toes. So he needed me to clip the toenails on his right foot. I understand I am responsible for fixing and repairing things, but toenails are not part of the job description! But, as a friend and fellow believer in the Lord, this was my one and only real job description—to love others, and the way I could express my love to Charlie, was to get down on my knees, grab his foot, and begin clipping.

This effort came from recalling the actions of Christ towards the disciples. In the Gospel of John, it was written, "Then (Christ) poured water into the basin, and began to wash the disciples' feet and to wipe them with the towel with which He was girded."[207] *(parentheses refer to author input)* Christ set a beautiful example for me to follow when He washed the disciples' feet. I knew, without doubt, that I was to get down on my knees in the apartment office and "wash" Charlie's feet. Sounds simple, but are we willing to display our devotion to the Lord through selfless acts of love? Christ explained to His disciples, "Truly, truly, I say to you, a slave is not greater than his master, nor is one who is sent greater than the one who sent him."[208]

The results of our relationship with the Lord Jesus Christ must be conveyed through love not only to Him, but also to our neighbors. For when we pursue God and others with love, the author of Hebrews confirmed that better things were to come for each one of us. He wrote, "For God is not unjust so as to forget your work and the love which you have shown toward His name, in having ministered and in still ministering to the saints."[209]

Let's face it. We must look at life with an eternal perspective. The apostle wrote to the Corinthian Church, "For we must all appear before the judgment seat of Christ, so that each one may be recompensed for his deeds in the body, according to what he has done, whether good or bad."[210] Let me reiterate that, with faith already placed in Christ, we are eternally saved. This judgment doesn't determine our salvation, but it does reveal the truth of eternal rewards that are waiting in heaven based on our service on earth. Paul wrote, "If any man's work which he has built on it remains, he will receive a reward."[211] People struggle with the mindset that we do things because of rewards, so please hear this … *overcome the mindset*! It is true that, as believers in the Lord, our essential goal in life is to please Him.[212] But as humans we need to be motivated for eternal rewards. When we are face to face with our Lord and Savior, we should want to hear the words, "Well done, good and faithful slave. You were faithful with a few things, I will put you in charge of many things; enter into the joy of your master."[213]

As citizens in America, we are bombarded with the freedom to choose the visible (a *temporal* faith), surrounded with the liberty to succeed (a *false* hope), and consumed with the opportunities to be accepted (a *deceiving* love). While we are U.S. citizens, we are also citizens of the heavenly kingdom, destined by the means of the Holy Spirit and absolute truth to believe in the one true God (an *eternal* faith), instructed to look for, and act upon, the promises of Christ (a *guaranteed* hope), and commanded to spur one another along (an *everlasting* love). If we desire our Christian lives to approach the throne of God in a glorifying and restored manner, we have no option but to live by these Christian virtues of faith, hope, and love.[214]

With an emphasis on faith, hope, and love, I am not pleading solely for a moral or social change within the body of Christ of America nor am I trying to offer up a formula for restoration. But I am indicating that faith, hope, and love will help direct us to a time of restoration during which we will be able to return to the Lord and draw near to Him. It is a combined effort, in which we will see the Lord work in our lives. As this day is drawing near, we must pray for "a spirit of wisdom and of revelation in the knowledge of Him."[215] Only then, with this spiritual insight from the Lord, will we begin to "walk in a manner worthy of the calling with which we have been called."[216] Therefore, as followers of Christ in America, let us cleanse our hands of the past and pursue our present life in Christ with an assured faith, an unwavering hope and a fervent love in order to *draw near to the Lord*.[217] Anything is possible with God.[218]

My entire being burns for the Lord and with this passion for restoration for the church in America. I am consumed with drawing near to the Lord. But even more so, I am absorbed with encouraging others to do the same. With so much of my life spent pursuing the American dream, I have now come to realize that there was some truth to what I was pursuing. Not all of it was bad. I was pursuing America, but over time and with growth, God began to clarify the specifics. Little did I know that the Lord was preparing me to pursue more than just a dream. He was training me to engage the believers of America and to make a significant impact in their spiritual lives. There is no denying it anymore. I wake up each and every morning with a heavy heart. At the same time, my mind is spinning with excitement. The Holy Spirit is working in my life to work in others' lives. I am committed—committed to revealing that a time of restoration must come. There is no turning back on this commitment. Many children growing up in a Christian home believe that America is a Christian Nation… not by *majority*, but *unanimously*. This is exactly what I pray for; that the childlike belief of a unanimously Christian Nation becomes a reality. This can only happen with the personal restoration of individual Christians and the complete awakening of the body of Christ in America.

CONCLUSION

One morning I unlocked the maintenance shop. With the fan humming at a medium speed, I sat in a cracked plastic chair, looking directly at my memory shelf of antique items and weathered license plates. I found myself mesmerized by all of the tools and equipment. A tube of DAP white caulk, an Ace red 4-in-1 screwdriver hung in its slot, an angled black paint brush was drip-drying on its peg hook, and a cordless DeWalt screwdriver rested on the wooden shelf. I like to have a clean and uniform look. My tools are basic, but they allow me to accomplish what I need.

That is exactly what the Lord has laid on my heart for this nationwide restoration. Simple, basic tools that get the job done. People get concerned when they hear the words "restoration," "revival" or "awakening." They think "weird." But to know the Lord in truth and experience Him in Spirit is exhilarating and, most definitely, unforgettable. Times of revival and restoration are designed by the Lord to be different and distinct from the norm. These times become the guiding, historic landmarks for church of America.[219] According to William Warren Sweet, revivals are known as "cascades in the stream of the church, recreating the main course of its waters."[220]

Each of us has already been given the essential tools and equipment needed to get through the day. Nothing complex, but with humility and prayer and fasting, we have been provided the means to come before the Lord on a daily basis. They also allow us to come together as a unified body of Christ in order to know and experience the transforming presence of Jesus Christ.

An Anglican Priest experienced a small revival in England and he confirmed his closeness with individuals who collectively experienced the Lord together:

> The more deeply people were involved, the more clearly was God calling them to go deeper still and to offer him the obedience of their whole lives . . . The diocese became a person, a body alive with a spirit . . . We experienced an extraordinary outburst of worship and happiness . . . We have seen reality break through like the sun through a fog, sweeping away the pretenses. People have been set free to become what they really are. We have begun to know that a whole diocese could be a fellowship of the Holy Spirit.[221]

My friends, we need the desire to draw near to the Lord. We need to adhere to the encouraging words of the prophet Hosea:

> Come, let us return to the Lord. For He has torn

> us, but He will heal us; He has wounded us, but He will bandage us. He will revive us after two days; He will raise us up on the third day, that we may live before Him. So let us know, let us press on to know the Lord. His going forth is as certain as the dawn; and He will come to us like the rain, like the spring rain watering the earth.[222]

When we truly desire restoration as the body of Christ, we will commit ourselves to a lifestyle of holiness. With this intentionality of living like Jesus, a divine response is inevitable as revival will rain down upon the land of the United States of America.

ORGANIZATION *for* REVIVAL

You are now aware that the spiritual walls of the church in America are being broken and tattered, and that the *time is now* to restore and rebuild them. Just as Nehemiah and the people of Judah recognized the walls of Jerusalem were torn down, we must collectively take action to rebuild the spiritual walls of the "church." Let's stop talking about it, discussing it and arguing about it. Let's just do it. Let's pursue revival.

Okay, so here is the blueprint to rebuild the ragged and worn-down spiritual walls of the American church. Two practicalities must happen. First of all, each and every believer must take ownership of this restoration process, specifically through an *organized time of prayer*. If we want change, let's pray for it as one body of Christ. We need to gather in one location and pray, not because we are being forced, but because we desire a change for our local church. Nehemiah knew, all too well, what it meant to personally long for restoration for his city and his people. For days he mourned, wept and fasted over the destruction of his city and his people. Yet, he took his desire to bring restoration to Jerusalem and turned it over to the Lord. Nehemiah cried aloud, "O Lord, I beseech You, may Your ear be attentive to the prayer of Your servant and the prayer of Your servants who delight to revere Your name, and make Your servant successful today and grant him compassion before this man."[223]

Prayer speaks volumes. When we want change, let's take it before the Lord. Prayer takes time, prayer requires effort and prayer demands energy. But all it takes is one Nehemiah in each city to take action and time to spearhead the corporate prayer. As an encouragement to other cities, I organized an effort to bring all of the various denominations of the "church in Dallas" together under one tent located downtown. We corporately prayed for one hour in the early morning of each day for forty straight days. For each of these forty days of prayer, there was a brief time of instruction based on a specific prayer found in Scripture. Then, with this specific prayer as a backdrop, the remainder of time was dedicated to allowing the Holy Spirit to move as the group prays for Dallas and the surrounding towns and cities.

Why forty days of prayer? To many, it seems like quite a commitment. Waking up early, driving to a central sight, meeting with others. *Exactly!* We need to reveal to the Lord that we are committed to seeing long-term change within our communities through the power of prayer. The actual number forty doesn't signify a magical formula. However, pastor Rick Warren stated, "The Bible is clear that God considers forty days a spiritually significant time period.

Whenever God wanted to prepare someone for his purposes, he took forty days:

> Noah's life was transformed by forty days of rain
> Moses was transformed by forty days on Mount Sinai
> The spies were transformed by forty days in the Promised Land
> David was transformed by Goliath's forty day challenge
> Elijah was transformed when God gave him forty days of strength from a single meal
> The entire city of Nineveh was transformed when God gave the people forty days to change
> Jesus was empowered by forty days in the wilderness
> The disciples were transformed by forty days with Jesus after His resurrection."[224]

Secondly, we need to come together and worship the Lord as a unified, yet *diverse body of Christ*. We need every person of every shape and size to corporately assemble together. We mustn't exclude individuals or groups of people because of their ethnic backgrounds. Jesus loves all people and all denominations. The red churches. The yellow churches. The black churches. The white churches. "We are all precious in His sight."[225] So let us sound the trumpet of restoration. The time is now for believers of all ethnic groups within each town and city to gather the people together.

In 1956, the Reverend Martin Luther King, Jr., addressed the Dexter Avenue Baptist Church in Montgomery, Alabama, with a sermon entitled, "Paul's Letter to American Christians." An essential point in Dr. King's sermon was the concentration of overcoming denominational barriers. Speaking figuratively as the apostle Paul, Dr. King said:

> Let me rush on to say something about the church. Americans, I must remind you, as I have said to so many others, that the church is the Body of Christ. So when the church is true to its nature it knows neither division nor disunity. But I am disturbed about what you are doing to the Body of Christ. They tell me that in America you have within Protestantism more than 256 denominations. The tragedy is not so much that you have such a multiplicity of denominations, but that most of them are warring against each other with a claim to absolute truth. This narrow sectarianism is destroying the unity of the Body of Christ. You must come to see that God is neither a Baptist nor a Methodist; He is neither a Presbyterian nor a Episcopalian. God is bigger than all of our denominations. If you are to be true witnesses for Christ, you must come to see that America.[226]

Just because the names on our physical buildings reveal Baptist or Brethren, Methodist or Presbyterian, doesn't excuse the biblical standard that we are *one* body. Paul reminded the Corinthian Church, "There may be no division in the body."[227] The "many members"[228] might have or display various gifts and purposes, but as the body of Christ, we are to keep our eyes upon Jesus Christ, the Head of our body. And, with Jesus as our central focus, the various denominations will be able to come together and pray as *one*.

Alongside the issues between denominations, Dr. King

furthered his thoughts on the church in America concerning the racial divide, when he said:

> There is another thing that disturbs me to no end about the American church. You have a white church and you have a Negro church. You have allowed segregation to creep into the doors of the church. How can such a division exist in the true Body of Christ? You must face the tragic fact that when you stand at 11:00 on Sunday morning to sing "All Hail the Power of Jesus Name" and "Dear Lord and Father of all Mankind," you stand in the most segregated hour of Christian America. They tell me that there is more integration in the entertaining world and secular agencies than there is in the Christian church. How appalling that is.[229]

Unfortunately, the truth speaks for itself. Our congregational gatherings in America are segregated. Many times, the division is because of geographic location. We attend church where we live. But let's overcome this distance barrier. Let's make the time, expend the energy, and put forth the effort to collectively worship together—*in one location as one body of Christ*. Specifically in Dallas, not only did we organize prayer for the forty mornings, but we are also organized forty different pastors and seven different worship teams to help lead us in worship for each of the forty evenings. Then, as we crossed the denominational streets and racial avenues in Dallas, the body of Christ began to see glimpses of a unified movement of the Holy Spirit all across the map. Let us each "put on the new self"[230] in Christ and experience a corporate renewal; "a renewal in which there is no distinction between Greek and Jew, circumcised and uncircumcised, barbarian, Scythian, slave and freeman, but Christ is all, and in all."[231]

Do you think that in order for the walls to be rebuilt in Jerusalem, Nehemiah could have done it by himself? No way! He needed the support and work of his fellow people of Judah to help bring the restoration process to the city. Together they overcame many obstacles: ridicule, mockery, threats, and fear. With the hand of God over their lives, the people were unified in their ultimate goal: *restoration!* The days were long and the times were tough, but each member of the supporting cast utilized their strengths and collectively made a difference. They wanted their city restored, and within fifty-two days, the wall was rebuilt. Praise God! Nehemiah wrote, "When all our enemies heard of it, and all the nations surrounding us saw it, they lost their confidence; for they recognized that this work had been accomplished with the help of our God."[232] In the past, God revealed Himself through His people. As Nehemiah of the past, and with the help of God, the body of Christ in America can bring glory to His name in the present. As the church in America, we must recognize the need to come together, collectively, as one body and pray for restoration.

Please refer to www.dallasrevival.org for more information (such as daily devotionals, sermons, video clips, etc . . .) on the 40-***day tent meeting that occurred near downtown Dallas during the spring of*** 2007.

WEEK 1[233]

DAY *1* Abraham's Prayer for Sodom
Genesis 18:20–33

DAY *2* Jacob's Prayer for Mercy from Esau
Genesis 32:6–12

DAY *3* Moses' Prayer at the Burning Bush
Exodus 3:1–4:18

DAY *4* Moses' Prayer After Crossing the Red Sea
Exodus 15:1–18

DAY *5* Moses' Prayer for Israel's Sin
Exodus 32:7–14

DAY *6* Moses' Second Prayer for Israel
Exodus 32:30–34

DAY 7 Moses' Prayer for God's Presence
Exodus 33:12–:34:9

WEEK 2

DAY *8* Moses' Prayer of Discouragement
Numbers 11:10–30

DAY *9* Moses' Prayer After the People Rebel
Numbers 14:10–20

DAY *10* Moses' 40 Day Prayer
Deuteronomy 9:18–29

DAY *11* Joshua's Prayer in Defeat
Joshua 7:2–15

DAY *12* Hannah's Prayer for a Child
1 Samuel 1:1–20

DAY *13* Hannah's Prayer of Thanksgiving
1 Samuel 2:1–10

DAY *14* David's Prayer of Praise for the Kingdom
2 Samuel 7:18–29

***WEEK** 3*

DAY *15* David's Praise for Deliverance
2 Samuel 22:1–51

DAY *16* Solomon's Prayer for Wisdom
1 Kings 3:4–15

DAY *17* Solomon's Prayer to Dedicate the Temple
1 Kings 8:22–61

DAY *18* Elijah's Prayer of Self-Pity
1 Kings 19:9–18

DAY *19* Hezekiah's Prayer for Deliverance
2 Kings 19:14–19

DAY *20* Hezekiah's Prayer for Healing
2 Kings 20:1–11

DAY *21* David's Prayer of Praise
1 Chronicles 17:16–27

***WEEK** 4*

DAY *22* David's Prayer at the People's Generosity
1 Chronicles 29:10–20

DAY *23* Jehoshaphat's Prayer in a Crisis
2 Chronicles 20:1–23

DAY *24* Ezra's Prayer for the Nation's Sins
Ezra 9:3–10:4

DAY *25* Nehemiah's Prayer for Jerusalem
Nehemiah 1:3–11

DAY *26* David's Prayer at His Son's Rebellion
Psalm 3

DAY *27* David's Prayer of Praise
Psalm 8

DAY *28* David's Prayer for a Pure Heart
Psalm 19

WEEK 5

DAY *29* David's Prayer to His Shepherd
Psalm 23

DAY *30* David's Prayer for Forgiveness
Psalm 51

DAY *31* David's Prayer for Guidance
Psalm 139

DAY *32* Isaiah's Prayer for Mercy
Isaiah 64:1–12

DAY *33* Jeremiah's Praise for God's Wisdom
Jeremiah 32:17–27

DAY *34* Daniel's Prayer of Confession
Daniel 9:4–19

DAY *35* Habakkuk's Prayer of Praise
Habakkuk 3:1–19

WEEK 6

DAY *36* The Lord's Prayer
Matthew 6:9–15

DAY *37* Jesus' Prayer for His Disciples
John 17

DAY *38* The Church's Prayer for Boldness
Acts 4:23–31

DAY *39* Paul's Prayer for the Ephesian Church
Ephesians 1:15–23; Ephesians 3:14–21

DAY 40 Prayers of Worship in Heaven
Revelation 11:15–19; Revelation 15:1–4; Revelation 16:5–7

PART II:

OVERVIEW *of* REVIVING *the* CHURCH

the DEFINITION *of* REVIVING *the* CHURCH

"Revival is not the discovery of some new truth. It's the rediscovery of the grand old truth of God's power in and through the Cross."[234]

- Sammy Tippit

"Therefore repent and return, so that your sins may be wiped away, in order that times of refreshing may come from the presence of the Lord..."

Acts 3:19

The body of Christ in America has become so comfortable and so secure in itself that it has been unwittingly plunged into a daily struggle with the figuratively deadly issue of complacency. Therefore, personal renewals are needed so each Christian will come to know and experience the Lord in a new and refreshing way on a daily basis. Lives will be changed when there is dependence upon the guidance of the Word of God and reliance on the Holy Spirit. Unlike any awakening of the past, restoration for the body of Christ in America must not be exclusive to just one area. On the contrary, if we desire to know and experience a corporate revival then we must be inclusive to all Christians, ranging from small churches that dot the countryside to large denominations on the east and west coasts. Lord willing, sweep across this nation and affect every small town and big city, every urban and suburban believer. When we come together, in collective and committed prayer, the Holy Spirit can sweep across this nation and awaken the entire body of Christ and cause non-believers to turn to Him. This revival can happen but only with a concentrated effort put forth by the church in America. It will not happen on any pre-determined timeline no matter how much we desire it. We are obligated to understand revival as it relates to Christianity in America, not through a definition in a dictionary, but through these six essential elements[235]:

> Revival is a sovereign act of God.
> Revival is a divine visitation.
> Revival is a time of personal humiliation, forgiveness, and restoration in the Holy Spirit.
> Revival has fearless preaching under the anointing of the Holy Spirit.
> Revival has the powerful presence of the Holy Spirit.
> Revival has changed communities and nations.

STAGES OF PROGRESSION ...

Short-Term Progression of awareness

Reviving the church can and will occur by bringing awareness to the followers of Jesus Christ of the importance of having a personal relationship with God through:

Understanding the importance of self-evaluation through the confession of personal and corporate sins.

Approaching the Lord in a time of personal fasting and prayer.

Identifying the need to keep our eyes on Jesus Christ.

Recognizing the relativity of revival through faith.

Mid-Term Progression of implementation

Reviving the church can and will occur when Christians are implementing our dependence on the truth and the Spirit into our daily lives through:

Exemplifying the attitude and lifestyle of Jesus Christ in our daily lives.

Actively fasting and praying corporately for a unified purpose—for the body of Christ to draw closer to the Lord.

Relying upon the Holy Spirit to know and experience a passionate and practical life-transformation.

Apply and implement a patient, steadfast perspective of eternal *hope.*

Long-Term Progression of impact

Reviving the church can and will occur when the disciples of Jesus Christ are impacting and encouraging others to know and experience the divine power of restoration through:

Impacting and encouraging others to sacrificially live for Jesus Christ.

Engaging in unceasing prayer of expectation.

Influencing and impacting the world in a disciplined manner which glorifies God.

Establishing and maintaining a relationship with others through *love.*

the VITAL REASONS *for* REVIVING *the* CHURCH

"Revival is that strange and sovereign work of God in which He visits His own people—restoring, reanimating, and releasing them into the fullness of His blessing."[236]

- Stephen Olford

Come, let us return to the Lord.
For He has torn us, but He will heal us;
He has wounded us, but He will bandage us.
He will revive us after two days;
He will raise us up the third day,
That we may live before Him.

Hosea 6:1–2

Throughout history, great nations have risen to power and then fallen by their own demise. It happened to the Babylonian Empire (625 to 539 BC), the Medo-Persian Empire (558 to 330 BC), the Grcco-Macedonian Empire (333 to 31 BC), and the all-powerful Roman Empire (31 BC–500 AD). In the last two centuries the world has witnessed the fall of Hitler's German Reich, the Austro-Hungarian Empire, Mussolini's Italian Empire, the Japanese Empire of Hirohito, the British Empire, and the USSR.[237] How do these nations rise and fall so easily? How can they go from being a flood of influence to a drop in the bucket? At one time, with an emphasis on *power*, these nations rose to the occasion; but with the underlying tone of *pride*, they crumbled to devastation. The city of Babel is an excellent example. The people wanted to "make a reputation for themselves," so they rebelliously took matters into their own hands.[238] They said, "Come, let us build for ourselves a city, and a tower whose top will reach into heaven, and let us make for ourselves a name, otherwise we will be scattered abroad over the face of the whole earth."[239] God was left out of their growth and developmental plans so the Almighty stopped the building of the tower and brought confusion to their language.

In light of historical and biblical examples, the United States of America must ask itself one simple question. As the economic and political power house of the world, are we to follow suit? While the Statue of Liberty stands tall and proud in the New York Harbor, America is quickly submerging its values in the waters of the Potomac. Why? Because we have gradually abused the blessings of liberty and freedom from the heaven above in order to strive for personal recognition and national gain. As Bill Bright described:

> We live in a nation that has lost its soul. Our abundance has led to greed. Our freedom has become license to turn away from God and pursue the role of the prodigal. Our national religious heritage is being forgotten or ridiculed as irrelevant or old fashioned.[240]

As members of the body of Christ in America, we are partially to blame. We have become so comfortable and so safe in our own environment that we have unwittingly plunged ourselves into a daily struggle with complacency. It seems we have forgotten that, at one time, our great nation based its daily decisions and actions on absolute Christian truths. We have forgotten what it means to impact and influence those around us because we are afraid to stand up and make a difference. We don't want to offend others who have different beliefs. We've grown to view God as an inconvenience and insult to others, rather than as the ultimate authority.

Let's face it, our nation is lost. The body of Christ has adjusted itself to the ways of its worldly neighbors. Who are we kidding? If revival does not occur within the body of Christ here in America, our nation will be no different than the other great nations that rose to power and fell to destruction. Moses wrote in Deuteronomy 8:19–20, "It shall come about if you ever forget the Lord your God and go after other gods and serve them and worship them, I testify against you today that you will surely perish. Like the nations that the Lord makes to perish before you, so you shall perish; because you would not listen to the voice of the Lord your God."[241] Jim Nelson Black in *When Nations Die*, wrote, "Could our own culture already be in the latter stages of decline? Is it possible that America—once universally acknowledged as the foremost economic and military power in the world—may one day, perhaps very soon go the way of Greece and Rome."[242] Until the body of Christ decides to whole-heartedly pursue revival for this nation, this demise will be the result of the United States of America.

As the late Bill Bright summarized in his book *The Coming Revival,* six indicators reveal that our nation's society is heading towards the path of national destruction.[243] Each indicator is prevalent today, and can no longer be overlooked:

> Removal of God in Society
>
> Constant attempts to remove God from the public schools, workplace, and holidays. Yet our nation was founded upon the Almighty God, just refer to the founding fathers of our great nation.
>
> So-called "Social Problems"
>
> Crime, violence, rape, abortion, AIDS, drug and alcohol addiction, etc. have become accepted as a norm within our society. Individuals that struggle and suffer with these issues are typically labeled and given a "justification" ticket to more trouble.
>
> Disintegration of the Traditional Family
>
> Divorce. It's running rampant in the American family. Broken homes are accepted and expected as family members give up on one another. The sense of family togetherness is all but lost.
>
> A Spirit of Selfishness
>
> The mindset and actions of "me-first" appear to be more prevalent than ever before. It is a "Me, Myself, and I" society.

Decisions of the Supreme Court

As the legal voice of this nation, the judicial system has taken certain matters into its own hands, such as separation of church and state, as well as abortion.

Homosexual "Explosion"

Enough is enough. The comparisons of Sodom and Gomorrah to the United States are, unfortunately, accurate. We must stop affirming the homosexual lifestyle as an accepted behavior within society.

> So let us know,
> let us press on to know the Lord.
> His going forth is as certain as the dawn;
> And He will come to us like the rain,
> Like the spring rain watering the earth.
>
> Hosea 6:3

the BENEFIT *of* REVIVING *the* CHURCH

"A spiritual awakening is no more than God's people seeing God in His holiness, turning from their wicked ways, and being transformed into His likeness."[244]

- Lewis Drummond

Revivals, unfortunately, are known and labeled as short periods of emotional highs. To some extent, this is a valid thought, but when we focus on these temporary emotions we are missing out on one huge benefit. We are able turn to the Lord for a natural integration of our beliefs into our daily lives. An ongoing life-transformation of our total being is *the* benefit of revival. Allow me to repeat it. *Life-transformation is the benefit of revival.* When we transform our lives to reflect the will of God, we reveal that "which is good and acceptable and perfect."[245] To experience the benefit of revival in our personal lives and within the body of Christ in America, we must look for a revitalization of our views towards the absolute truths which can only be found in the Scriptures. That is, when our life-transforming perspective can begin to weave absolute truths into a biblical worldview. This biblical worldview will testify to our own personal life-transformation and bring us closer to living our lives within the will of God.

However, within the church in America, when there appears to be a lack of knowledge of Scripture, a biblical worldview rarely exists. According to the Barna Group, only 4% of the adults polled in 2003 hold to a biblical worldview.[246] So how will we ever see the benefits of a revival if we don't hold a biblical worldview? The pollster George Barna confirmed this concerning question when he said:

If Jesus Christ came to this planet as a model of how we ought to live, then our goal should be to act like Jesus. Sadly, few people consistently demonstrate the love, obedience and priorities of Jesus. The primary reason that people do not act like Jesus is because they do not think like Jesus. Behavior stems from what we think—our attitudes, beliefs, values and opinions.

Although most people own a Bible and know some of its content, our research found that most Americans have little idea how to integrate core biblical principles to form a unified and meaningful response to the challenges and opportunities of life. We're often more concerned with survival amidst chaos than with experiencing truth and significance.[247]

Revival can and will occur when Christians in America accept ownership of the absolute truths … and more importantly, hold to them. This is when we will begin to witness the *benefit* of revival in our own lives. So what does a biblical worldview consist of? According to The Barna Group, a biblical worldview contains six specific views upheld by the sixty-six books within the Holy Bible.[248] They are:

1. Jesus Christ lived a sinless life
   2 Corinthians 5:21; Hebrews 4:15;
   Hebrews 7:26;1 Peter 2:21–24; 1 John 3:5
2. God is the all-powerful and all-knowing Creatoroftheuniverseand Hestillrulesittoday
   Isaiah 40; Jeremiah 10:11–13;
   Romans 1:18–20, 8:28–30; 2 Peter 1:3
3. Salvation is a gift from God and cannot be earned
   Acts 13:38–39; Romans 5:1; Galatians 2:16; Ephesians 2:8–9; Titus 3:7
4. Satan is real
   Matthew 4:1–11; John 8:44; 2 Corinthians 4:4; Ephesians 2:2, 6:10–17; Revelation 12:9
5. A Christian has a responsibility to share their faith in Christ with other people
   Matthew 24:14; Matthew 28:19–20; Acts 1:8; Romans 10:15; 2 Corinthians 5:20
6. The Bible is accurate in all its teachings
   Psalm 119:105; Acts 2:42; 2 Timothy 3:16–17; 2 Peter 1:19–21; 2 Peter 3:2

When these absolute truths are revitalized in our own lives, the ongoing benefit of having a life-transformation is right around the corner. Not only will we understand how Scripture practically affects our decisions and actions, but we will also impact others around us. Change is contagious when it is authentic and real. People will notice and want to know the source of our different lifestyle. That is one way that revival will occur in many communities. It starts with willing and able individuals who want to make a difference for the kingdom of God in their own lives.

When we hold a biblical worldview, the life-transformation benefit is ongoing. We will walk securely. We will not stumble. We will not fear. The Lord will be our confidence.[249] Life-transformation develops a stronghold based in our own personal walk with the Lord even when we are tempted and tested. This life-transformation will carry over into surrounding communities.

Life-transformation is an ongoing benefit that we might not be able to articulate well and understand in our own lives until we have personally experienced it. When we do, there is a sense of peace and joy. There is a sense of direction. The local body of Christ will become like-minded, and the community will become unified ... to bring glory to the name of God.

The benefit of personal *life-transformation* through a biblical worldview allows each of us to impact those around us because we are ... [250]

A. 31 times less likely to accept cohabitation
2% versus 62%

B. 18 times less likely to endorse drunkenness
2% versus 36%

C. 15 times less likely to condone gay sex
2% versus 31%

D. 12 times less likely to tolerate profanity
3% versus 37%

E. 11 times less likely to describe adultery
4% versus 44%

F. 78 times less likely to accept pornography
.5% versus 39%

G. 92 times less likely to accept abortion
.5% versus 46%

> As the number of true saints multiplied... the town seemed to be full of the presence of God: it was never so full of love, nor of joy, and yet so full of distress as it was then. There were remarkable tokens of God's presence in almost every house. It was a time of joy in families on account of salvation being brought unto them... On whatever occasions person met together, Christ was heard of and seen in the midst of them... The Spirit of God began to be so wonderfully poured out in a general way through the town, people had soon done with their old quarrels, backbitings, and intermeddling with other men's matters. The tavern was soon left empty. Every day seemed in many respects like a Sabbath day. [251]
>
> \- Jonathan Edwards
> on the Spirit moving in his community of
> Northampton, Massachusetts, 1735

the CONSEQUENCE *of* NOT REVIVING *the* CHURCH

"If revival is being withheld from us it is because some idol remains still enthroned; because we still insist in placing our reliance in human schemes; because we still refuse to face the unchangeable truth that, 'It is not by might, but by My Spirit.'"[252]

\- Jonathan Goforth

I know you inside and out, and find little to my liking. You're not cold, you're not hot—far better to be either cold or hot! You're stale. You're stagnant. You make me want to vomit.

You brag, "I'm rich, I've got it made. I need nothing from anyone," oblivious that in the fact you're a pitiful, blind beggar, threadbare and homeless …

Revelation 3:15–17, *The Message*

> Think about it. There is nothing like a refreshing, cold glass of water when we are hot and thirsty. There is nothing like a steaming hot shower when we have just come in from the bitter cold. People rarely like lukewarm water. It is not cold, and it is not hot. Typically, drinking lukewarm water gives off a certain taste that we immediately want to spit out. Now place the church in America in one of these three categories:
>
> 1) hot
> 2) cold
> 3) lukewarm

Will we honestly identify the category we as a body of Christ are in? If so, I think it would be fair to say that overall, we give "half-hearted efforts (as) self-satisfied Christians ..."[253] We are lukewarm. Why? It is because we have become comfortable and content with our material and our wealth. We tend to believe that we need more stuff: more money, more cars, bigger homes—more of everything but the Lord. We are being deceived into a comfortable, lukewarm lifestyle, and we don't even know it. This is the consequence of not pursuing revival. As the deceiver of the whole world,[254] Satan is active and present. He has made us think and believe we are a rich nation, but through the eyes of eternity, we are spiritually poor. And if we don't pursue personal and corporate revival, we will always remain in the vomit-inducing state of being lukewarm. Throughout the Gospels and Revelation, Christ described this lukewarm spiritual state as: "wretched, pitiful, poor, blind, and naked."[255]

The apostle Paul warned us not to be ignorant of Satan's schemes and strategies.[256] Until we put forth energy and effort in our relationship with the Lord, nothing will change in our personal lives—absolutely nothing. Therefore, if we are not willing to obey or listen,[257] how do we expect the Lord to work in our own lives on a daily basis? It won't happen. Even though Christ has won for us the gift of eternal life, Satan will continue to rule over our earthly lives if we don't change from this lukewarm lifestyle. God is willing to work with His body of believers that we might reject the ways of Satan, but we must first be willing to recognize our own spiritual apathy.

How much longer can the body of Christ maintain this lukewarm spiritual pace? If it were up to Satan, we would remain in this lukewarm state until kingdom come, and God is no longer glorified. We are riding the fence of spirituality, which has its consequences. According to the Gospel of Mark, we are to be "lamps on a stand."[258] We are not to hide it or, worse yet, preserve it. As the church in America, we tend to conserve our spiritual energy; and as the founder of Campus Crusade for Christ, Bill Bright, confirmed, we have become an impotent body of Christ in America. We have surrounded ourselves with the temptations of easy living; where the consequences are already in full effect. Unfortunately, we are not aware of this problem. So we must shed light on the situation. Christ must be evident in our lives. Therefore, until a life-transformation occurs, the consequence of being lukewarm will continue.

As a result of no revival in the past century, Bill Bright listed a few observations that have already occurred:[259]

1. Christians have left their first love.

   Based on attitudes and actions, a spiritual fervor

is missing within the body of Christ. It is time to return to our love for the Lord and others.

2. Christians, for the most part, are sorely divided.
Let's face it, Sunday mornings are the most segregated time in the week. With thousands of denominations, the church in America appears to be divided with their own distinct beliefs.

3. Christians often reflect a poor image.
The bottom line is, if we are going to talk the talk, we need to walk the walk. Too many times, we appear to be modern-day Pharisees who expect others to uphold a standard that we fail to uphold ourselves.

4. Christians have lost their influence on society
If evangelical Christians have so much of an influence on our nation, then why is our society steeped in constant crime and violence? Could it be that we are those "who call themselves Christians [but] are really not Christians at all; although religious, … never experienced a personal relationship with Jesus Christ?"

5. Christians are searching for easy solutions and quick success
To many Christians, the desired result is to bring heath and wealth into their own lives. It is preached by televangelists, and dispersed like a vending machine. Insert a prayer, and God will give you everything you want.

6. The "Church" is weakened by a "what's-the-use?" mentality
   The mindset is, since we know that the world is going to get worse before it can get better, we simply don't put forth effort towards others. After all, Christ told us things would get this bad.

7. The "Church" has become culturally conditioned
   One simple question: can you tell the difference between a believer and a non-believer?

> The people I love, I call to account—prod and correct and guide so that they'll live at their best. Up on your feet, then! About face! Run after God …
> Are your ears awake? Listen. Listen to the Wind Words, the Spirit blowing through the churches.
>
> Revelation 3:19,22 *The Message*

the ENEMY *and* HIS GOALS

"There is no neutral ground in the universe; Every square inch, every split second, is claimed by God and counter-claimed by Satan."[260]

- C.S. Lewis

As believers in Jesus Christ we are at war—a spiritual war—that the body of Christ in America has chosen to overlook. How can such an oversight take place? It has done so because we are either unable to recognize it, or too uncomfortable to identify our real adversary.

Currently, Satan is the prince of this world[261] and he roams and walks the earth.[262] He is not observing us from his ornate throne, surrounded by the damned and by lakes of Hell-fire; he is here, walking among us. He is an active adversary looking to attack each of us as followers of Jesus

Christ. The apostle Peter confirmed Satan's desire to destroy us when he wrote in his first letter, "Be of sober spirit, be on the alert. Your adversary, the devil, prowls around like a roaring lion, seeking someone to devour."[263]

Can we see our enemy? Do we actually know where our struggles come from? Do we really understand why life can be so devastating? Are we clear as to why we are faced with mockery and suffering? Do we completely comprehend why it is that we fall? Why we fail and give in to temptations? These are tough questions... with only one answer. Satan. He is our enemy, our adversary, and his ultimate goal in this spiritual war is to bring destruction to the kingdom of God.

Our perception of Satan is construed. We identify Satan as a mix between man and demon. Satan is usually portrayed as fiery red with two horns, a forked tongue, and a pointy tail. We dress like him in Halloween costumes and even name athletic teams after him. Worse is that we categorize him as a *symbolic* figure of evil rather than the *absolute* evil that he truly is. In fact, according to The Barna Group, 46% of all born-again adults believe that Satan does not exist.[264] He is simply a figurative representation of the dark side. This is a prime example of how Satan, very effectively, uses deception as a weapon against us. He wants us to believe that he is simply a symbol of evil (as current culture portrays him to be). Why? Because when we do not understand the reality of our enemy, we underestimate the role that he plays in each of our lives.

In the very beginning,[265] Satan was an anointed angel, given responsibility to oversee the Garden of Eden.[266] However, he decided to go against the seal of perfection, and was filled with violence.[267] Remember when Adam and Eve ate the forbidden fruit from the Tree of Knowledge of Good and Evil? Satan used his power and wisdom to turn

Adam and Eve away from God.[268] Satan also corrupted other angels, swaying them to join in rebellion[269] against God. Some of these fallen angels are permanently bound in the Abyss,[270] while some are temporarily on the loose. These "angels on the loose" are known as demons[271] that work side by side with Satan and strive to bring destruction to the kingdom of God. With his destructive mentality, one of Satan's goals is to "rob God of His glory and man of his joy."[272] Satan does not want God to be glorified. Nor does Satan want us to worship the one and only God. A spiritual war is being waged: God and His faithful followers vs. Satan and his demons.

If we can recognize and identify the role that Satan tries to play in each of our lives, we will be better able to engage in spiritual warfare. Paul wrote, "For our struggle is not against flesh and blood, but against the rulers, against the powers, against the world forces of this darkness, against the spiritual forces of wickedness in the heavenly places."[273] Please do not deny the impact that Satan tries to have in our lives on a daily basis. We must know who we are up against, and know that Satan disguises himself in many ways and plays many roles.

Satan is:

Abaddon / Apollyon (angel of the abyss)
Revelation 9:11

Adversary (an opponent)
1 Peter 5:8

Accuser (against one in the assembly)
Revelation 12:10

Devil
Matthew 4:1

Enemy (adversary)
Matthew 13:39

Evil One (hurtful)
Matthew 13:19; Matthew 13:38

Father of Lies and Murderer (falsifier)
John 8:44

god of this world
2 Corinthians 4:4

prince of the power of the air
Ephesians 2:2

ruler of this world
John 12:31

Satan (opponent)
Job 1:6

son of perdition/destruction
John 17:12; 2 Thessalonians 2:3

Tempter
Matthew 4:3; 1 Thessalonians 3:5

Despite the cunning and widespread influence of Satan, praise be to God, Satan's freedom to rule over the world will not last. At the return of Jesus Christ, Satan will be bound for 1,000 years.[274] Then, for a short period of time, Satan will be released and he will make one final attempt to deceive the nations from all four corners of the earth.[275] Satan knows his time is limited, for God has prepared an eternal fire for the devil and the demons.[276] Satan, demons and those who oppose God "will be tormented day and night forever and ever."[277]

Until the Day of the Lord arrives, we must persevere and hold fast in each and every spiritual battle against Satan and his fallen demons. We have no choice. Satan will not stop until he has either been destroyed or he has fulfilled his goal, bringing destruction to the kingdom of God. As believers in Jesus Christ, we already know the outcome of this spiritual war. Satan and his rebellious goals have already been defeated.

> Death is swallowed up in victory.
> O death, where is your victory? O death, where is your sting?
> The sting of death is sin, and the power of sin is the law;
> but thanks be to God, who gives us the victory through our Lord Jesus Christ.
>
> 1 Corinthians 15:54–56

the STRATEGY *for* REVIVING *the* CHURCH

"We cannot organize revival, But we can set our sails to catch the wind from Heaven When God chooses to blow upon His people once again."[278]

- G. Campbell Morgan

A Clear Strategy for Revival: As individuals of the church in America, *let us* recognize that we need to return to the Lord. As certain as the dawn of each morning, God is ready and willing to prepare our path of restoration. He will pour Himself onto our lives, like the rain watering the earth.[279] We must press on without hesitation, that we might better know and experience Him.

The body of Christ in America must integrate a strategy that involves the pursuit of four integrated paths. Each has a separate objective but together they lead to a unified restoration for all of America:

1. Concentration of *humility.*
2. Focus on *prayer & fasting.*
3. Being extraordinary through *holiness.*
4. Results from *divine response.*

SUMMARY OF RESTORATION

"Concentrated focus brings extraordinary results."[280]

Objective: To restore the body of Christ in America to its original foundation by means of humility, prayer and fasting, holiness, and divine response.

To achieve this objective we encourage the body of Christ to:

Be aware of how important your relationship with God is in your lives.

Implement and integrate your dependence on the truth and Spirit into your daily lives.

Impact and encourage others to know and experience the divine power of restoration.

the CONDITIONS *for* REVIVING *the* CHURCH

"Revival is a 'renewed conviction of sin and repentance, followed by an intense desire to live in obedience to God. It is giving up one's will to God in deep humility.'"[281]

- Charles Finney

HUMILITY

In pursuit of *concentration*

Objective: To concentrate the body of Christ in America at the foot of the cross so they, as followers of Jesus Christ, would humbly and sacrificially distinguish themselves from the ways of the world.

To achieve this objective we encourage the body of Christ to:

> *Understand the importance of self-evaluation through the confession of personal and corporate sins.*
>
> *Exemplify the attitude and lifestyle of Jesus Christ in your daily lives.*
>
> *Impact and encourage others to sacrificially live for Jesus Christ.*

PRAYER & FASTING

In pursuit of *focus*

Objective: To progressively focus the body of Christ in America with prayer and fasting through the lives of individuals, as well as collectively come before the Lord to seek restoration.

To achieve this objective we encourage the body of Christ to:

> *Approach the Lord in a time of personal fasting and prayer.*
>
> *Actively fast and pray corporately for a unified purpose—for God to bring. about a nationwide restoration*
>
> *Engage in unceasing prayer of expectation.*

HOLINESS

In pursuit of being *extraordinary*

Objective: To increase the spiritual growth and development of the body of Christ in America so that we constantly reflect the image of God in our daily lives and, by example, draw others closer to Him.

To achieve this objective we encourage the body of Christ to:

Identify the need to keep our eyes on Jesus Christ.

Rely upon the Holy Spirit to know and experience a passionate and practical, life-transformation.

Influence and impact the world in a disciplined manner which glorifies God.

DIVINE RESPONSE

In pursuit of *results*

Objective: To further the daily pursuit of the spiritual virtues of faith, hope, and love of the church in America, so we personally experience the hand of God working in our lives as we victoriously march through the stages of life.

To achieve this objective we encourage the body of Christ to:

Recognize the relativity of revival through faith.

Apply and implement a patient, steadfast perspective of eternal hope.

Establish and maintain a relationship with others through love.

APPENDIX

PERSONAL DOCTRINE *of* SALVATION

As ***a follower of Jesus Christ***, I *believe* the foundation in which I entrust the eternal state of my life is straightforward and simple. I am either destined to eternity in the unquenchable fire of hell[282] or granted everlasting life in the kingdom of God.[283] Unfortunately, from the beginning I was inherently headed down the wrong path as a result of Adam's sin in the Garden of Eden.[284] Immediately, I was placed under the penalty of sin,[285] where any action I carried out constantly fell short of pleasing God.[286] Even worse, the wages of this sin led to death[287] with no promise or hope for the future. Yet, by the unconditional grace of God,[288] I have been saved[289] from this eternal damnation and been given eternal life. This gift of salvation from God the Father is exactly what it implies, it is free and it is a gift. I did nothing to earn or deserve being saved from the wrath of God.[290] But gratefully, out of His love for me,[291] God the Father substituted His one and only Son to die on the cross as a result of my sin[292] so I may not perish. Therefore, to understand this reconciliation of my life back to God through the death of Christ,[293] the only requirement to believe and accept this gracious gift is through the saving power of faith in Jesus Christ.[294]

As ***a follower of Jesus Christ***, I *believe* that by faith alone, I understand, agree, and trust[295] that Jesus is the Christ, and as the Son of God, He has granted eternal life to me through the power of His name.[296] With having been justified by faith alone,[297] I believe my personal relationship with Jesus Christ does not rely on nor require any unnecessary additions to be saved. Additions such as repentance,[298] public confession of Christ,[299] baptism,[300] church membership, and continual good works[301] are indicators of saving faith, but are not mandatory to spend eternity with the Almighty God.[302]

As ***a follower of Jesus Christ***, I *believe* to have faith based on the absolute truth according to the Scripture,[303] in which I am assured of my salvation. This same absolute truth reveals and assures me I have been born-again into a new creature; where the old has gone, and the new has come.[304] With this life-changing transformation through the blood of Jesus, I am confidently able to approach the Holy God in full assurance of faith.[305] Simultaneously, upon the immediate justification of faith in Christ, assurance of salvation has been poured out upon me through the regeneration and renewing of the Holy Spirit in my life.[306] I have been given the Spirit of Christ,[307] which allows me to abide in Him[308] and attempt to live a life that displays spiritual fruit.[309]

As ***a follower of Jesus Christ***, I *believe* this daily outcome of our faith in Jesus Christ and walking by the Spirit, in which we unconditionally love and serve Him with all of our heart, soul, and mind,[310] is known as the process of sanctification. However, this pursuit of daily holiness can occur once it follows the initial justification of faith. Only then, in sanctification, will spiritual disciplines such as reading Scripture, prayer, fasting, love for others, evangelism, acts of service, etc.[311] transpire into a God-honoring lifestyle. But this sanctified lifestyle will never obtain perfection until the perfect state of glorification in heaven. For as long as I am on earth, my body will always remain dead to sin, but the spirit of righteousness given to me will continue to remain alive.[312]

As ***a follower of Jesus Christ***, I *believe* the Lord God, in His sovereign plan and purpose, currently exemplified since the foundation of the earth my eternal state in which I was already determined not by anything I had done, but solely by the power and mercy of God. I was drawn to Christ by the power of God.[313] Therefore, since I was predestined to be adopted as a son of Jesus Christ,[314] according to His will, God will never abandon a child of His. Even when I continue to return to my old, sinful way of living, God is greater than all, and He will never let me perish.[315] Because of this free gift of salvation immediately given to me through faith, I have been granted a secure future for eternity to come. An eternal security which can only come from having confidence in Jesus Christ, who will in His sovereignty continue His faithful work in my life until the day He returns.[316]

PERSONAL DOCTRINE *of* HOPE DURING END TIMES

As ***a follower of Jesus Christ***, I *believe* I am to confidently hold fast to the blessed hope which I have been given through the faithful promise of Jesus Christ.[317] For, as surely as the Son of God died on the cross and rose again on the third day, I am assured that my Lord and Savior will come again and receive me into heaven which He has prepared.[318] Whether I am alive on earth or have died and fallen asleep in Jesus,[319] I am encouraged from the word of the Lord that in the twinkling of an eye,[320] I can be caught up in the clouds to meet with Christ and remain with Him always.[321] As I eagerly await for His imminent return, I must remain attentive to my faith in Christ as well as provide comfort and support to others[322] with this message of eternal hope.

As ***a follower of Jesus Christ***, I *believe* that the believers of Christ will be rescued from the wrath to come.[323] At an unknown time, the prophetic fulfillment of Israel's seventieth week will occur.[324] During the first half of this seven-year tribulation, the Anti-Christ himself will establish a peaceful covenant with Israel and the surrounding nations. However, before the final three and a half years of the tribulation, the Anti-Christ will break the Middle-East agreement. Peace will no longer exist and the abomination of desolation will rush upon the earth immediately.[325] Darkness will enter, and the day of the Lord will come like a thief in the night.[326] Christ referred to this time of judgment as the great tribulation.[327] Since the beginning of time, nothing like this tribulation has ever occurred, nor will it ever occur again. Therefore, all believers who accepted Christ during this seven-year timeframe and survived, which will include the 144,000 Jewish witnesses[328] and tribulation saints[329], will be encouraged to flee from Jerusalem into the mountains. For the wrath of God and this time of tribulation will continue until the return of Jesus Christ.

As ***a follower of Jesus Christ***, I *believe* in these last days of difficult times,[330] the second coming of Christ will draw an end to the ungodliness.[331] The Messianic King will return to earth just as He ascended into heaven. And with His second coming, the King of kings and Lord of lords[332] will rule His kingdom with dominion and power over all of mankind. The King who is Faithful and true[333] will send the deceitful Anti-Christ and false prophet alive into the lake of fire.[334] Also, as per the Word of God, Christ will strike down the nations[335] in order to welcome the entire earth into the millennium. Most importantly, in this time period that will last one thousand years, Satan will be bound and thrown into the abyss,[336] where he will no longer be able to rule as the prince of the power of the air.[337] With Christ now having fulfilled the prophetic role as the Davidic king forever,

God will complete the Abrahamic and Mosaic covenantal promises. Restoration will be brought to the land of Israel.[338] Israel will be saved from the Deliverer, and all of mankind will recognize and seek the Lord.[339]

As ***a follower of Jesus Christ***, I *believe* once the thousand years have passed, Satan will be released from the abyss, and will gather all the nations from the four corners of the earth.[340] With people too numerable to count, the devil of deceit will lead his army to surround the holy city of Jerusalem to battle the saints. However, according to the divine Scriptures, the Lord will intervene and send His fire upon the earth in order to devour the opposing army before there is any fighting. The infamous battle of the end times will not be much of a battle and upon the destruction of his innumerable army, Satan will be immediately tossed into the lake of fire, where he will be tormented day and night forever[341] along with the Anti-Christ and the false prophet.

As ***a follower of Jesus Christ***, I *believe* the next eschatological step for myself and all other Christians will be to inherit and obtain eternal righteousness before the great white throne of God. All of humanity, through all of the ages, dead or alive at the time, Christian or non-Christian, will be required to go before this eternal judgment. At this seat of sovereignty, God will determine whose names have been written in the book of life. I believe if a person has chosen not to obey the gospel of Jesus Christ, their name will not be found in the book of life.[342] They will be cast into the lake of fire, a physical location where there will be no relief from the eternal agony of the flame.[343] The unbelievers will be placed in eternal destruction, away from the presence of the Lord.[344] But for those of us whose names the Lord has found in the book of life, because we have chosen to believe in Jesus Christ, we will all be granted eternal life in the new heaven and new earth. These will be an eternal place in which all things have been made new and where death and pain no longer exist.[345] I will be glad and rejoice in the Almighty God who has established His sovereignty in this new heaven and new earth from the beginning until the very end.[346] I will finally be at my eternal home, and my desire to be with Him will be fully satisfied.[347] No longer will I have to deal with the ongoing struggle of sin; on the contrary, I will be set free from sin as a new and glorified child of God.[348]

BIBLIOGRAPHY

acknowledgements

1 Psalm 92:1 NASB

2 Proverbs 31:25 NASB

table of contents

3 Bush, President George W., Rough Outline taken from National Strategy for Victory in Iraq, http://www.whitehouse.gov/infocus/iraq/iraq_strategy_nov2005.html, November 2005.

the backdrop

4 Psalm 78:70–72 NASB (New American Standard Bible)

5 Habakkuk 2:3 THE MESSAGE

restoration

6 Deuteronomy 4:29 THE MESSAGE

7 *Jesus, Joy of Man's Desiring*, www.suite101.com/article/cfm/lutheranism/44214., November 2005.

8 Hosea 5:15 NASB

9 Hosea 5:14 NASB

10 Hosea 6:1 NASB

11 Psalm 63:1 NASB

12 Barna, George, The Barna Group, *Born Again Christians Just As Likely to Divorce As Are Non-Christians,* http://www.barna.org/FlexPage.aspx?Page=BarnaUpdate&BarnaUpdateID=170, *December* 2005.

13 Barna Group, The Barna Group, *Born Again Adults Remain Firm in Opposition to Abortion and Gay Marriage,* http://www.barna.org/FlexPage.aspx?Page=BarnaUpdate&BarnaUpdateID=94, December 2005.

14 Falwell, Jerry, "Remembering the 46 Million," *Falwell Confidential–Inside Weekly Newsletter*, August 12, 2005.

15 Luke 16:19–31 NASB

16 Luke 17:11–21 NASB

17 *Global Poverty, What is Poverty?* http://www.netaid.org/global_poverty/global-poverty, December 2005.

18 *Issues - AIDS,* http://www.one.org/issues, December 2005.

19 Hosea 6:1–3 NASB

20 Hosea 6:16 NASB

21 Walvoord, John F., ed., *The Bible Knowledge Commentary*, Hosea 6:1–3, p.1393.

22 Radmacher, Earl., ed., *Nelson's New Illustrated Bible Commentary*, Hosea 6:1–3, p.1031.

23 Eph 4:1–3 NASB

24 Barna, George, The Barna Group, *Born Again Adults Remain Firm in Opposition to Abortion and Gay Marriage,* http://www.barna.org/FlexPage.aspx?Page=BarnaUpdate&BarnaUpdateID=94, December 2005.

25 Radmacher, Earl., ed., *Nelson's New Illustrated Bible Commentary*, 2 Timothy 3:16–17, p.1616–1617.

26 Ibid.

27 2 Timothy 3:16–17 NASB

28 1 Thessalonians 1:5 NASB

29 Ibid.

30 John 14 :26 NASB

31 1 Corinthians 2:10–16 NASB

32 Galatians 5:22–23 NASB

33 John 4:24 NASB

34 Hosea 6:3 NASB

35 Deuteronomy 11:11–15 NASB

36 Exodus 34:34–35 NASB

humility

37 Psalm 66:18 NASB

38 Lamentations 5:21 NASB

39 Finney, Charles G., *Revivals of Religion*, p.33–34.

40 Psalm 42:1–2 NASB

41 1 Peter 2:9–10 THE MESSAGE

42 1 Kings 19:10, 18 NASB

43 Bono, U2–*How to Dismantle an Atomic Bomb*–"All Because of You," http://www.christianitytoday.com/music/glimpses/2004/howtodismantleanatomicbomb.html, January 2006.

44 Isaiah 58:15 THE MESSAGE

45 Philippians 2:2 NASB

46 Philippians 2:3 NASB

47 Radmacher, Earl., ed., *Nelson's New Illustrated Bible Commentary*, Philippians 2:1–13, p.1549.

48 Psa 51:10–13 NASB

49 Radmacher, Earl., ed., *Nelson's New Illustrated Bible Commentary*, Philippians 2:1–13, p.1549.

50 Romans 12:10 NASB

51 Philippians 2:4–5 NASB

52 Radmacher, Earl., ed., *Nelson's New Illustrated Bible Commentary*, Philippians 2:1–13, p.1549.

53 Graham, Billy, *Revival in Our Time,* p.77.

54 Ephesians 4:20–24 *The Message*

55 Romans 12:1–2 NASB

56 Philippians 2:6 NASB

57 Lightner, Robert P., *The Bible Knowledge Commentary*, Philippians 2:5–8, p.654.

58 Ibid.

59 Mark 10:45 NASB

60 Philippians 2:7 NASB

61 Deuteronomy 6:5 NASB

62 Galatians 2:20 NASB

63 Philippians 2:9–10 NASB

prayer & fasting

64 Severns, Sarah, "Holland Tunnel Dream," journal entry, January 14, 2006.

65 Arena, Kelli, "N.Y. tunnel plot uncovered," http://www.cnn.com/2006/US/07/07/tunnel.plot/index.html, July 2006.

66 Ibid.

67 Drummond, Lewis, *The Awakening that Must Come,* p.44–45.

68 Joel 2:12 NASB

69 Radmacher, Earl., ed., *Nelson's New Illustrated Bible Commentary*, Joel 2:12–17, p.1043.

70 Ibid.

71 Joel 2:13–14 NASB

72 Psalm 80:2–3 NASB

73 Psalm 51:10–12; Romans 15:16; 1 Corinthians 6:11; Galatians 5:22–23 NASB; 1 Thessalonians 1:5–6; Titus 3:5

74 John 4:24 NASB

75 Joel 2:15–17 NASB

76 Chisholm, Jr., Robert B., *The Bible Knowledge Commentary*, Joel 2:12–17, p.1417.

77 Radmacher, Earl., ed., *Nelson's New Illustrated Bible Commentary*, Joel 2:12–17, p.1043.

78 Constable, Dr. Thomas, "Joel," http://www.soniclight.com/constable/notes/pdf/joel.pdf, p.12. , March 2006.

79 Piper, John, *A Hunger for God: Desiring God Through Fasting and Prayer*, pp.22–23.

80 Piper, John, *A Hunger for God: Desiring God Through Fasting and Prayer*, pp.23.

81 Matthew 9:15 NASB

82 Schaeffer, Edith. The Life of Prayer (Wheaton: Crossway Books, 1992), pp.75–76.

83 Joel 2:17 NASB

84 1 Peter 2:9–10 NASB

85 Chadwick, Samuel., as quoted by Leonard Ravenhill, *Revival Praying*, p.44.

86 Drummond, Lewis, *The Awakening that Must Come*, p.121.

87 Isaiah 44:3 NASB

88 Ravenhilll, Leonard. *A Treasury of Prayer*, p.52.

89 2 Chronicles 7:14 NASB

90 1 Thessalonians 5:17 NASB

91 Matthew 7:7–11 NASB

92 Grassmick, John D., *The Bible Knowledge Commentary*, Mark 11:22–24, p.1230.

93 Mark 11:22–24 NASB

94 Radmacher, Earl., ed., *Nelson's New Illustrated Bible Commentary*, Matthew 7:7–11, p.1153.

95 Barbieri, Jr., Louis, *The Bible Knowledge Commentary*, Matthew 7:7–11, p.34.

96 John 14:12–14 NASB

97 Matthew 6:9–13 NASB

98 Joel 2:18–27 NASB

99 Joel 2:28–29 NASB

extraordinary results

100 Marshall, Randy, pastor at Dallas Bible Church, Dallas, TX.

holiness

101 Ephesians 1:4 THE MESSAGE

102 Dieter, Melvin Easterday., ed., *Five Views on Sanctification* (Grand Rapids, MI: Academie Books, 1987), 70.

103 Harrison, Everett Falconer., ed., *Baker's Dictionary of Theology* (Grand Rapids,' Baker Book House, 1960), 258.

104 Luke 5:8 NASB

105 Lowery, David K., *The Bible Knowledge Commentary*, 2 Corinthians 4:16–5:10, p.564–565.

106 2 Corinthians 4:18 NASB

107 Colossians 3:1–2 NASB

108 Robertson, A.T., *Word Pictures in the New Testament*, 4:500.

109 **"AT&T, Ford Focus and U.S. Army signed as tour sponsors"** http://www.hostcommunications.com/0,6032,1_1422_0_15864,00.html, July 2006.

110 Havner, Dr. Vance, *The Quotable Christian*, www.pietyhilldesign.com/gcq/quotepages/holiness.html, July 2006.

111 James 1:17 NASB

112 James 4:14 NASB

113 Colossians 3:3–4 NASB

114 Ibid.

115 Geisler, Norman L., *The Bible Knowledge Commentary, Colossians*, p.679–683.

116 Stott, John R. W., *Men Made New: An Exposition of Romans 5–8*, 1st ed. (Chicago, Inter-Varsity Press, 1966), 34.

117 Colossians 3:5–8 THE MESSAGE

118 Ephesians 4:1 NASB

119 Ephesians 4:19 NASB

120 Ephesians 4:20 NASB

121 Colossians 3:9–11 THE MESSAGE

122 Ephesians 4:20–21 NASB

123 Ephesians 4:22 NASB

124 2 Corinthians 5:17 NASB

125 Hall, Cheryl, "Promotion Power: The Marketing Arm muscles its way to top of industry with innovative campaigns," *The Dallas Morning News*, http://www.dallasnews.com/sharedcontent/dws/bus/columnists/chall/stories/DN-Hall_07bus.ART.State.Edition1.187662d2.html, July 2006.

126 2 Timothy 1:8–9 NASB

127 Lewis, C.S., *The Quotable Christian*, www.pietyhilldesign.com/gcq/quotepages/holiness.html, July 2006.

128 Ephesians 4:23–24 NASB

129 Colossians 3:12 NASB

130 Paraphrase of Colossians 3:12–14 NASB

131 Colossians 3:12–14 THE MESSAGE

132 Dieter, Melvin Easterday., ed., *Five Views on Sanctification*. Grand Rapids, MI: Academie Books, 1987, 220.

133 Ibid.

134 Dieter, Melvin Easterday., ed., *Five Views on Sanctification* (Grand Rapids, MI: Academie Books, 1987).

135 Geisler, Norman L., *The Bible Knowledge Commentary, Colossians*, p.680.

136 Philippians 2:12–13 NASB

137 Marshall, Randy, pastor at Dallas Bible Church, Dallas, TX.

138 Dieter, Melvin Easterday., ed., *Five Views on Sanctification*. Grand Rapids, MI: Academie Books, 1987, 215.

139 Packer, J.I., *Keep in Step with the Spirit* (Old Tappan, N.J.: F.H. Revell, 1984), 109.

140 Hebrews 12:14 NASB

141 Packer, J.I., *Keep in Step with the Spirit* (Old Tappan, N.J.: F.H. Revell, 1984), 111.

142 Mark 12:30 NASB

143 Gal 5:22–23 NASB

144 Matthew 28:19–20 NASB

145 Acts 19:10 THE MESSAGE

146 Paraphrase of Professor Howard Hendricks, Dallas Theological Seminary

147 Acts 1:8 NASB

148 Colossians 4:4 NASB

149 Colossians 4:5 NASB

150 Colossians 4:6 NASB

151 Matthew 25:35–37 THE MESSAGE

152 Colossians 3:17 NASB

153 Dieter, Melvin Easterday., ed., *Five Views on Sanctification*. Grand Rapids, MI: Academie Books, 1987, 160.

154 1 John 3:2 NASB

155 Dieter, Melvin Easterday., ed., *Five Views on Sanctification*. Grand Rapids, MI: Academie Books, 1987, 89.

divine response

156 Joshua 4:7 NASB

157 Radmacher, Earl., ed., *Nelson's New Illustrated Bible Commentary*, Joshua 4:1–9, p.278–279.

158 Hebrews 6:1–3 THE MESSAGE

159 Hebrews 6:4–8 THE MESSAGE

160 Hodges, Zane C., *The Bible Knowledge Commentary*, Hebrews 6:9–12, p.796–797.

161 Hebrews 6:9 NASB

162 Ibid.

163 FAITH…

SAVING FAITH - Galatians 2:15–16; Ephesians 2:8–9 NASB

ACTIVE FAITH - 2 Corinthians 5:7; Hebrews 11:1–40; James 1:2–8 NASB

164 HOPE in…

GOD - Psalm 39:7; Psalm 71:14; Romans 12:12 NASB

RESURRECTION - Acts 24:15 NASB

BLESSED/LIVING HOPE - Titus 2:13; 1 Peter 1:3–5, 13; Romans 15:13 NASB

165 LOVE...

Deuteronomy 6:4–9; 1 Samuel 20:17 NASB

Matthew 22:37; Mark 12:30; Luke 10:27 NASB

John 13:1–20; 1 Corinthians 13:1–13 NASB

166 DRAW(ING) NEAR...

Psalm 69:16–19; Psalm 119:145–152; Hebrews 4:16; Hebrews 7:18–19, 25; Hebrews 10:19–25; James 4:8 NASB

167 FELLOWSHIP...

1 Corinthians 1:9; 1 John 1:3; 1 John 1:5–10 NASB

168 THE PRESENCE OF THE LORD...

Hebrews 10:19 NASB

169 Hebrews 10:22 NASB

170 Hebrews 11:1 THE MESSAGE

171 Hebrews 6:9 NASB

172 Marshall, Randy, pastor at Dallas Bible Church, Dallas, TX.

173 1 Thessalonians 1:3 NASB

174 James 2:14–18 THE MESSAGE

175 Hebrews 6:12 NASB

176 Thurston, Mabel N., *The Adventure of Faith,* p.14–15.

177 Mark 8:11–12 NASB

178 Job 1:1 NASB

179 Job 1:6–12 NASB

180 Job 1:21 NASB

181 Judges 6:14 NASB

182 Judges 6:36–40 THE MESSAGE

183 Thurston, Mabel N., *The Adventure of Faith,* p.19.

184 1 Thessalonians 1:3 NASB

185 Thurston, Mabel N., *The Adventure of Faith.*

186 Hebrews 6:12 NASB

187 Elwell, Walter A., ed., "Hope," *Baker Theological Dictionary of the Bible*, p.355.

188 Philippians 3:20 NASB

189 Romans 15:4 NASB

190 Hebrews 6:18 NASB

191 Hebrews 6:18 NASB

192 1 Peter 2:20 NASB

193 Hebrews 6:11 NASB

194 Hebrews 3:6 NASB

195 1 Peter 1:3–5 NASB

196 King. Jr., Dr. Martin Luther,. "Paul's Letter to American Christians." http://www.stanford.edu/group/King/sermons/561104.000_Paul's_letter_to_American_Christians.html, September 2006.

197 *Commitment*, http://groups.yahoo.com/group/dailybreaddevotions2/message/6540; 11/30/05; author unknown., July 2006.

198 Hebrews 10:23 NASB

199 Black Eyed Peas, *Where is the Love?*, http://www.lyrics007.com/Black%20Eyed%20Lyrics/Where%20Is%20The%20Love%20Lyrics.html, June 2006.

200 Jude 1:21 NASB

201 Elwell, Walter A., ed., "Love," *Baker Theological Dictionary of the Bible*, p.494.

202 1 John 3:18–19 THE MESSAGE

203 Colossians 3:14a NASB

204 Colossians 3:14b NASB

205 Holland, Ben and Lindsay, former Swissaire Apartments' tenants

206 Hebrews 10:24–25 NASB

207 John 13:5 NASB

208 John 13:16 NASB

209 Hebrews 6:10 NASB

210 2 Corinthians 5:10 NASB

211 1 Corinthians 3:9 NASB

212 2 Corinthians 5:9 NASB

213 Matthew 25:23

214 FAITH, HOPE & LOVE

Romans 5:1–5; 1 Corinthians 13:13; Galatians 5:5–6; Ephesians 1:15–19; Ephesians 4:1–6; Colossians 1:2–6; 1 Thessalonians 5:8; Hebrews 6:9–12; Hebrews 10:19–25; 1 Peter 1:1–9; 1 Peter 1:20–23 NASB

215 Ephesians 1:15–19 NASB

216 Ephesians 4:1–6; Philippians 1:27–28 NASB

217 Hebrews 10:19–25; James 4:8 NASB

218 Matthew 19:26; Mark 10:27; Luke 1:37; Luke 18:27 NASB

conclusion

219 Mode, Peter G., *The Frontier Spirit in American Christianity* (New York: Macmillan, 1923), 41.

220 Sweet, William Warren, *Revivalism in America* (New York: Charles Scribner's Sons, 1944), xv.

221 Verney, Stephen, *Fire in Coventry* (Westwood, N.J. Fleming H. Revell, 1964), 24, 26, 35, 36, 51.

222 Hosea 6:1–3 NASB

organization for revival

223 Nehemiah 2:11 NASB

224 Warren, Rick, *The Purpose Driven Life* (Grand Rapids: Zondervan, 2002), 9–10.

225 Lyrics from *Jesus Loves the Little* Children, http://www.christianindex.org/1130.article.printl, September 2006.

226 King. Jr., Dr. Martin Luther,. "Paul's Letter to American Christians." http://www.stanford.edu/group/King/sermons/561104.000_Paul's_letter_to_American_Christians.html, September 2006.

227 1 Corinthians 12:25 NASB

228 1 Corinthians 12:20 NASB

229 King. Jr., Dr. Martin Luther,. "Paul's Letter to American Christians." http://www.stanford.edu/group/King/sermons/561104.000_Paul's_letter_to_American_Christians.html, September 2006.

230 Colossians 3:10 NASB

231 Colossians 3:11 NASB

232 Nehemiah 6:16 NASB

prayer schedule

233 Denton, Bill., *Developing Students of the Bible*, http://www.atlantaroad.org/praayers.html., August 2006.

the definition of revival

234 Tippit, Sammy, *Quotes about Revival*, http://www.goodpassage.com/quotes_about_revival.htm, December 2005.

235 Bright, Bill. "Revival Fires" in *The Coming Revival*, http://www.thegreatawakenings.org/revivalfires.htm, December 2005.

the vital reasons for revival

236 Olford, Stephen, *Quotes about Revival*, http://www.goodpassage.com/quotes_about_revival.html, December 2005.

237 Ames, Richard F. *Rise and Fall of Nations*, http://www.tomorrowsworld.org/cgi-bin/tw/tw-mag.cgi?category=Magazine19&item=1104108822, December 2005.

238 Walvoord, John F., ed., *The Bible Knowledge Commentary*, Genesis 11:104, p. 44.

239 Genesis 11:4 NASB

240 Bright, Bill. "America Under Judgment," in *The Coming Revival*, http://www.thegreatawakenings.org/americanunderjudgment.htm, December 2005

241 Deuteronomy 8:19–20 NASB

242 Ames, Richard F. *Rise and Fall of Nations*, http://www.tomorrowsworld.org/cgi-bin/tw/tw-mag.cgi?category=Magazine19&item=104108822, December 2005.

243 Bright, Bill. "America Under Judgment" in *The Coming Revival*, http://www.thegreatawakenings.org/americanunderjudgment.htm, December 2005

the benefit of revival

244 Drummond, Lewis, *Quotes about Revival*, http://www.goodpassage.com/quotes_about_revival.htm, December 2005.

245 Romans 12:1–2 NASB

246 Barna, George. "A Biblical Worldview Has a Radical Effect on a Person's Life," Dec.1, 2003, http://www.barna.org/FlexPage.aspx?PageUpdate&BarnaUpdateID=154, December 2005.

247 Ibid.

248 Ibid.

249 Proverbs 3:23 NASB

250 Barna, George. "A Biblical Worldview Has a Radical Effect on a Person's Life," Dec.1, 2003, http://www.barna.org/FlexPage.aspx?Page=BarnaUpdate&BarnaUpdateID=154, December 2005.

251 Ibid.

the consequence of no revival

252 Goforth, Jonathan, *Quotes about Revival*, http://www.goodpassage.com/quotes_about_revival.html, December 2005.

253 Radmacher, Earl. ed., *Nelson's New Illustrated Bible Commentary*, Revelation 3:17, p. 1740.

254 Revelation 12:9 NASB

255 Walvoord, John F., ed. *The Bible Knowledge Commentary*, Revelation 3:17, p. 940.

256 2 Corinthians 2:11 NASB

257 Bright, Bill. "The Impotent Church" in *The Coming Revival*, http://www.thegreatawakenings.org/theimpotentchurch.htm, December 2005.

258 Mark 4:21 NASB

259 Bright, Bill. "The Impotent Church" in *The Coming Revival*, http://www.thegreatawakenings.org/theimpotentchurch.htm, December 2005.

the enemy and his goals

260 Lewis, C.S., *Quotes about Revival*, http://www.goodpassage.com/quotes_about_revival.html, December 2005.

261 John 12:31 NASB

262 Job 1:7 NASB

263 1 Peter 5:8 NASB

264 Barna, George. "Beliefs: Trinity, Satan," http://www.barna.org/FlexPage.aspx?Page=Topic&TopicID=6, December 2005.

265 1 John 3:8 NASB

266 Ezekiel 28:12–19 NASB

267 Ezekiel 28:12–18 NASB

268 Genesis 3 NASB

269 Revelation 12:4,9 NASB

270 Luke 8:31 NASB

271 Matthew 25:41 NASB

272 Pocock, Dr. Michael. WM525 Spiritual Warfare, Dallas Theological Seminary, Fall 2003; The Sources of Spiritual Opposition: Satan and Demons.

273 Ephesians 6:12 NASB

274 Revelation 20:1–3 NASB

275 Revelation 20:7–9 NASB

276 Matthew 25:41 NASB

277 Revelation 20:10 NASB

the strategy for revival

278 Morgan, G. Campbell, *Quotes about Revival*, http://www.goodpassage.com/quotes_about_revival.html, December 2005.

279 Paraphrase of Hosea 6:1–3 NASB

280 Radmacher, Earl. ed., *Nelson's New Illustrated Bible Commentary*, Acts 19, p. 1406.

the conditions for revival

281 Shelhamer, E.E., *How to Experience Revival*, (Springdale, PA: Whitaker House, 1984, p.7)

personal doctrine of salvation

282 **HELL**, Mark 9:43

283 **KINGDOM OF HEAVEN**, Psalm 145:13, Luke 12:32

284 **THE FALL OF MAN**, Genesis 3:15, 1 Chronicles 1:1, Luke 3:38, Romans 5:12–14

285 **UNDER SIN,** Romans 3:9

286 **ALL HAVE SINNED**, Romans 3:23

287 **PENALTY OF SIN**, Romans 6:23

288 **GRACE OF GOD**, Ephesians 2:8

289 **SALVATION**, Acts 16:31

290 **PROPITIATION/WRATH OF GOD**, John 3:36, Romans 5:9 , Ephesians 5:6, Hebrews 2:17, 1 John 2:2

291 **LOVE OF GOD**, John 3:16 - Romans 5:8

292 **SUBSTITUTION**, Matthew 20:28, Mark 10:45

293 **RECONCILIATION**, Romans 5:10, 2 Corinthians 5:18–21

294 **FAITH ALONE**, Ephesians 2:8–9

295 **SAVING FAITH**

J. Scott Horrell, *"The Nature of Saving Faith"* (Dallas Theological Seminary, Spring 2005), Unpublished class notes in ST104 Soteriology.

296 John 1:12, John 20:31

297 **JUSTIFICATION**, Galatians 2:16, Ephesians 3:17

298 **REPENT/REPENTANCE**

299 J. Scott Horrell. "The Nature of Saving Faith," 2. Luke 22:32, Acts 26:18, Hebrews 6:1

PUBLIC CONFESSION OF CHRIST

J. Scott Horrell, "The Nature of Saving Faith," 3., Romans 10:9–10

300 **BAPTISM**

J. Scott Horrell, "The Nature of Saving Faith," 3., Acts 2:38, Mark 16:16

301 **GOOD WORKS**

J. Scott Horrell, "The Nature of Saving Faith," 3.

302 2 Corinthians 4:5, James 2:14–17

J. Scott Horrell, "The Nature of Saving Faith," 3.

303 **ASSURANCE OF FAITH**

304 J. Scott Horrell, "The Nature of Saving Faith," 7., 2 Corinthians 5:17, Ephesians 4:22–24, Colossians 3:9–10

305 Hebrews 10:22

306 **EVIDENCE OF HOLY SPIRIT**

J. Scott Horrell, "The Nature of Saving Faith," 9–10, Titus 3:5–6

307 Galatians 4:6

308 1 John 4:13

309 **EVIDENCE OF SPIRITUAL FRUIT**

J. Scott Horrell, "The Nature of Saving Faith," 10., 2 Corinthians 13:5, Galatians 5:22–25

310 **SANCTIFICATION**, Mark 12:30, Leviticus 19:2, Hebrews 10:10 , Hebrews 12:10

311 Horrell, J. Scott, "The Nature of Saving Faith," 10.

312 Romans 8:9–11

313 **PREDESTINATION**

314 John 6:44, 65, Ephesians 1:3–5,11

315 **ETERNAL SECURITY**

J. Scott Horrell, "The Nature of Saving Faith," 16–17., John 10:27–29, Hebrews 7:25,

316 Philippians 1:6

personal doctrine of during end times

HOPE

317 Heb 10:23

318 John 14:1–3

319 1 Thessalonians 4:13–15

320 1 Corinthians 15:51–52

321 1 Thessalonians 4:16–17

322 1 Thessalonians 4:18

TRIBULATION

323 1 Thessalonians 1:10, 1 Thessalonians 5:9

324 Daniel 9:27

325 Daniel 11:27

326 1 Thessalonians 5:1–2

327 Matthew 24:15–21

328 Revelation 14:1

329 Revelation 14:12

SECOND COMING OF CHRIST/MILLENIUM

330 2 Timothy 3:1–5, 1 Timothy 4:1–3

331 Isaiah 11:9, Jeremiah 30:7

332 Revelation 19:16

333 Revelation 19:11

334 Revelation 19:20

335 Revelation 19:15

336 Revelation 20:1–3

337 Ephesians 2:1–2

338 Acts 15:16–17

339 Romans 11:25–27

340 Revelation 20:7–9

THRONE OF JUDGMENT

341 Revelation 20:10

342 Revelation 20:11–15

343 Luke 16:19–26

344 2 Thessalonians 1:7–9

NEW HEAVENS AND NEW EARTH

345 Revelation 21:4

346 Isaiah 65:17–19

347 Philippians 3:20

348 Romans 8:19–23

With direction from God, encouragement from family and friends, and plenty of perseverance, Kyle Lance Martin has one true passion—reviving others in their relationship with Jesus Christ. Disheartened by the lack of impact of Christianity, he strives to articulate the absolute truth for others to understand and apply. Kyle is currently pursuing a doctorate at Gordon-Conwell Theological Seminary, studied at Dallas Theological Seminary graduating with an M.A. in Biblical Studies, and Taylor University where he obtained a bachelor's degree in Business Administration. He and his wife, Laura, live in Dallas with their daughters, Maya and Nadia, where Kyle recently transitioned from serving as property manager of an apartment complex to Pastor of Discipleship and Revival at Dallas Bible Church.